BOSTON MARATHON
TRADITIONS & LORE

BOSTON MARATHON TRADITIONS & LORE

PAUL C. CLERICI

THE
History
PRESS

Published by The History Press
Charleston, SC
www.historypress.com

Front cover, top left: Four-time Boston Marathon winner Bill Rodgers and his wreath from 1975. *Photo by Paul Clerici*; *top middle*: Boston Marathon finisher medals, dating to the first year in 1983. *Courtesy Ashworth Awards*; *top right*: Lit spires of the Pablo Eduardo–created Boston Marathon Marker Memorial on Boylston Street. *Photo by Paul Clerici*; *bottom*: Early Boston Marathon finish lines included a single white line on Exeter Street, as in 1935, with a victorious Johnny "The Elder" Kelley. *Courtesy of the Boston Public Library, Leslie Jones Collection.*

Back cover, top: *Boston Herald-Traveler* photographer Leslie Ronald Jones (*standing*), at the BAA press vehicle, 1938. *Courtesy of the Boston Public Library, Leslie Jones Collection*; *inset*: Gold-dipped olive-branch champion wreath. *Photo by Paul Clerici.*

First published 2024

Manufactured in the United States

ISBN 9781467155977

Library of Congress Control Number: 2023949474

I dedicate this book to my late parents, Frank Clerici Sr. and Carol Hunt-Clerici; my late brother, David Clerici; and my brother, Frank Clerici Jr.

CONTENTS

FOREWORD

In the realm of athletic achievement, few sporting events hold the same hallowed status as the BAA Boston Marathon. This iconic race and test of endurance, which winds through the historic streets of eight cities and towns, is much more than a mere sporting event; it is a living testament to the indomitable spirit of human endurance and perseverance, the very embodiment of tradition and celebration of the thousands of stories that shape its legacy.

From its very inception in 1897, following the first Modern Olympic Games in Greece in 1896, the Boston Marathon stood out not only for its athletic competitiveness but also for its deeply ingrained traditions. The very date of the race—Patriots' Day—was deliberately chosen to coincide with the State of Massachusetts's holiday that commemorated the Battles of Lexington and Concord, marking the beginning of the American Revolution.

Similarly, the race course itself was modeled and laid out to closely replicate the original 1896 Olympic Marathon course, from the small town of Marathon to the ancient Olympic stadium in the city of Athens. This alignment of history and sport reinforced the marathon's significance as a strong signal of determination and resilience, shared by runners, volunteers, and spectators alike.

When I was hired in late 1984 by then-president Tom Brown of the Boston Athletic Association Board of Governors to help save and restore the prestige and financial security of the venerable Boston Marathon, it was unclear if the decades-old race would even survive. Sounds incredible to some, impossible to many. Cast against the strength and popularity of today's Boston Marathon, it's hard to believe such was ever the case. But sadly, it indeed was. Imagine a situation where there was no staff, no office, no sponsorship, no prize money, and a deep-rooted fear of progress and resistance to change.

The turmoil, frustrations, and litigation of the late 1970s and early 1980s are well documented, but why did so many people care so much about this decidedly old running event? What's so special about it? Certainly the many years of exciting local and international competition were a part of it. Yet it was no different than many other marathons around the country at the time. What is it about this event that makes believers out of so many—runners, volunteers, spectators, the eight communities through which the race is contested? Clearly, it's the personal stories of perseverance and triumph, the unique local traditions, and the generations of relationships that set the Boston Marathon apart from all others.

During my long career at the BAA, and still today as a member of the Board of Governors, it was my singular obligation, as steward of this most impactful event, to identify solutions, develop a strong organization, move the Marathon forward, and protect all that was special about this great race. And above all, be mindful to "do no harm." With that as my overarching motto, I set out to address the challenges facing the Marathon, including building a strong team of leaders and collaborating with the BAA Board and many partners in the community, to bringing a sense of pride back to all those who had supported this great race through the decades.

Securing sponsorship was one of the first orders of business so that prize money would be available to attract the elite athletes once again. Signaling a major first step, our groundbreaking 10-year sponsorship partnership with John Hancock Mutual Life Insurance Company would not only allow for such a radical change but also mean moving the finish line closer to their headquarters in Copley Square—at the time a major, yet very necessary, change to improve the race in so many ways. This radical departure meant moving the finish from The Prudential Center, where it had been for 21 years, from 1965 to 1985, hosting many historic finishes, including Bill Rodgers's and Joan Benoit Samuelson's historic wins on the Pru's Ring Road. Even though the start and finish lines of the Marathon had moved many times over the years, this necessity was not without resistance.

The finish line, however, had to move to its present location, on Boylston Street near the Boston Public Library (close to Copley Square and the former John Hancock Tower). Any further movement eastward would have resulted in the start line in Hopkinton being pulled from out of the Town Green area and down the steep slope toward Ashland. This became one of many prime examples of progress and collaboration while respecting the traditions of the storied race course.

As the years have passed, the Marathon continued to evolve while staying true to its important traditions, which speak to its uniqueness and place in the world of sport. Progress, with respect, was our mantra. The inclusivity of the race was expanded, welcoming athletes from all walks of life and abilities and all corners of the globe. And without compromising the competitiveness of the race, we established the Boston Marathon as an extremely important fundraising partner for hundreds of local nonprofits. An important win-win for the Marathon and the communities that sustain it, I am most proud of the Boston Marathon charity program, which has raised over $500 million to date, and counting.

Paul Clerici's long and successful history of detailing and celebrating road races, and the characters behind them, has led to a real appreciation of the particularly rich history of the Boston Marathon. That appreciation extends to the many players in the presentation of this great event. Through his keen knowledge of the sport's many contributors and countless interviews, Paul has the unique ability to honor, respect, and write about the origins of the customs and traditions that make up all that the Marathon represents.

This book explores some of these customs and uniquely Boston traditions. Paul takes a deep dive into many of the functions and relationships that have developed over many years, decades actually, that make the Marathon so much more than just a road race. What's so special about the winners' olive wreaths, the finisher medals, the start and finish lines? The amazing evolution of this great event is on display here, from the generations of athletes, the unsurpassed media coverage, and the varied collection of monuments along the course in celebration of the race's deep history, to the worldwide partnerships and cultural interactions that help to define its legacy.

I learned early on in my role as leader, defender, and steward, that the Boston Marathon is not a single-day event but a continuous narrative that intertwines the past, the present, and the future. Whether you run in the footsteps of the generations before you, volunteer along the course, or spectate in support, as many have done for well over one hundred years, you become a part of the history and very fabric of the Marathon and its legacy. "Boston" is a true celebration of human potential, the very Olympic spirit from which it was born and a testament to the power of tradition, unity, and strength in the face of challenges and adversity.

Foreword

This book is a must-read for all fans of the Boston Marathon, as it clearly helps highlight the Marathon's storied history while making more meaningful the truly remarkable experience of every individual who participates in, or contributes to, this annual celebration of sport and community.

Guy Morse III
BAA Board of Governor
BAA CEO/Executive Director (2000–10)
Boston Marathon race director (1985–2000)

ACKNOWLEDGEMENTS

I would like to thank everyone who contributed their stories and photos; gave of their time for interviews; and offered their overall assistance and support, which helped me make this a fun, entertaining, and informative book.

Guy Morse III, for his insightful and engaging foreword, powered by his institutional knowledge and love of the Boston Marathon. Photograph consultant Christine Lee, for her always-reliable expertise and advice.

AAIM, AIMS, Michael Alfano, Alpha Omega Council, Megumi Amako, Nicholas Arciniaga, ARRS, Dan Ashworth, Ashworth Awards, Attleboro City Hall, BAA, Brian Baker, Will Belezos, Rich Benyo, Dr. Cheri Blauwet, *Boston Globe*, *Boston Herald*, BPL Digital Commonwealth (especially Danielle Pucci and Monica Shin), Ambrose "Amby" Burfoot, Gina Caruso, Mike Chamberas, Bill Chenard, the Consulate General of Greece in Boston, Dr. John Coyle, Alistair Cragg, Diane Culhane, Bob Cullum, Alan Culpepper, Neil Cusack, Rob de Castella, David Donahue, Elva Dryer, Massachusetts governor Michael Dukakis, Emerson College, Marc Fein, Joann Flaminio, Shalane Flanagan, Jack Fleming, Jessica Gauthier, Roberta "Bobbi" Gibb, Tom Grilk, Kyle Grimes, Ryan Hall, Amanda Hansen, Kiyokatsu Hasegawa, Massachusetts governor Maura Healey, Yoshibumi Honda, Kay Horiuchi, Eric House, Dick Hoyt, Rick Hoyt, *Huffington Post*, Lisa Hughes, James Hurley, IOC (especially Andrew Mitchell, Emmanuelle Moreau, Rachel Rominger, and Sandrine Tonge), Edward Jacobs, Kevin Johnson, Leslie Ronald Jones, Deena Kastor, Meb Keflezighi, Johnny "The Elder" Kelley, Johnny "The

Younger" Kelley, Tim Kilduff, Nicholas Kourtis, Howard Kramer, Dimitri Kyriakides, Jacques "Jack" LeDuc, Peter Lemonias, Tommy Leonard, Robert Levitsky, Desiree Linden, Pat Lodigiani, Chris Lotsbom, Mark Lund, Burke Magnus, *Marathon & Beyond*, Kayla McCann, Tatyana McFadden, Dave McGillivray, Alvaro Mejia, Greg Meyer, Lorraine Moller, Bill Morris, Guy Morse III, North Attleborough Town Hall, NYRR, Dr. Michael O'Leary, Ome Marathon, Masaru Otake, Christos Panagopoulos, Uta Pippig, John Powers, Constance "Connie" Prescott, Gloria Ratti, Toni Reavis, Roger Robinson, Bill Rodgers, *Runner's World*, Joan Benoit Samuelson, Nancy Agris Savage, Bill Sayman, Marc Schpilner, Jan Colarusso Seeley, Brian Sell, Mary Kate Shea, Miharu Shimokado, Doug Small, Geoff Smith, Kim Smith, Massachusetts Senate president Karen Spilka, Bill Squires, Kathrine Switzer, Symeon Tegos, The History Press, TRACS Inc., Fred Treseler, Freddie Treseler IV, Walpole Public Library, and Nina Wang.

For research and historical reference, *The B.A.A. at 125: The Official History of the Boston Athletic Association, 1887–2012* by John Hanc and the Boston Athletic Association (Sports Publishing, 2012); *Boston Marathon Media Guide* by Boston Athletic Association (B.A.A., 2023); *Boston Marathon: Year-By-Year Stories of the World's Premier Running Event* by Tom Derderian (Skyhorse Publishing, 2017); *The Genuine Works of Flavius Josephus the Jewish Historian, Translated from the Original Greek, According to Havercamp's Accurate Edition*, by William Whiston (London, 1737); *Official Report of the Games of the I Olympiad, Athens, 1896: The Olympic Games B.C. 776–A.D. 1896: First Part, The Olympic Games in Ancient Times* by SP. P. Lambros and N.G. Polites, edited by Charles Beck, English translation by A. v. K. Athens, *Second Part, The Olympic Games in 1896* by Pierre de Coubertin, Timoleon J. Philemon, N.G. Polites, Charalambos Anninos, English translation by A. v. K. Athens (H. Grevel and Co., 1897; Courtesy LA84 Foundation Digital Library Collection, Los Angeles, California); *Olympia: Gods, Artists and Athletes* by Ludwig Drees, English translation by Gerald Onn (Pall Mall Press, 1967; IOC); *The Olympic Games in Ancient Greece* by general supervisor Nicolaos Yalouris (Ekdotike Athenon S.A., 1982; IOC); *The Theoi Project: Greek Mythology* website, Auckland, New Zealand (Aaron J. Atsma, 2000–11).

INTRODUCTION

At about 40 kilometers (24.5 miles), the first competitive marathon was held on March 10, 1896, in Greece, followed by the first Modern Olympic Games Marathon, also in Greece, on April 10, 1896. Later in the fall, on September 19, 1896, the first marathon on American soil was run from Stamford, Connecticut, to Columbia Circle in New York City, for its only time. And on Patriots' Day, Monday, April 19, 1897, just 13 months after the very first marathon ever run, the inaugural Boston Marathon (American Marathon) was held, from Ashland to Boston, in Massachusetts.

The Boston Athletic Association (BAA), founded in 1887, sent several athletes on the U.S. team for the 1896 Games of the I Olympiad in Athens, Greece. One of the events, the marathon, resonated with the BAA members, who subsequently brought back the idea to Boston to incorporate it into their own multievent BAA Games.

Like no other annual marathon footrace, Boston (eventually 26.2 miles) has decades of accumulated traditions and lore that each year continue to attract runners worldwide.

Since 1897, in addition to cheering on their own family and friends, and of course the leaders, spectators often would not consider the race over until they saw the likes of several legendary participants beyond their athletic peak but who still represented the pride and spirit of the Boston Marathon. Some of those iconic athletes included 1924 U.S. Olympic Marathon bronze medalist and seven-time Boston champion Clarence DeMar; two-time U.S. Olympian and two-time Boston winner Johnny "The Elder" Kelley, who started 61 and finished 58, between 1928 and 1992; the Team Hoyt father-son duo of Dick Hoyt pushing his son Rick Hoyt—diagnosed with spastic cerebral palsy—in a custom-fit wheelchair; and even, albeit more toward the evening hours, Dave McGillivray, the Boston Marathon race director who each year traditionally begins his race several hours after the official start and then often finishes at night.

Participants also look forward to the many traditions and lore along the course: huge crowds, media personnel, hovering helicopters "Where It All Starts" in Hopkinton; cheers from front-yard parties and restaurants, the late "official dog" golden retriever Spencer in Ashland; block parties, same-day Red Sox game updates, musicians performing atop a car dealership building in Framingham; Santa Claus, fishermen along Lake Cochituate in Natick; the Scream Tunnel of cheering Wellesley College students in Wellesley; boisterously supportive spectators along the Newton hills, including Heartbreak Hill, and Boston College students in Newton and Brighton; yells of encouragement on the Beacon Street rolling hills in Brookline; the final mile of support in Kenmore Square to that righthand turn onto Hereford Street and lefthand turn onto Boylston Street; and the displays of Marathon Daffodils in Boston.

There are many other traditions and lore, of course, including the addition of divisions for push-rim wheelchair (male in 1975; female in 1977), duo (first recognized in 1981 with Team Hoyt), visual impairment (1986), handcycle (exhibition in 2001), and para athletic (2021) participants—of varying abilities and levels of amateur and elite status—that have continued the BAA's ongoing endeavor for inclusion.

"The Boston Marathon has a rich history of inclusion, dating back to the 1970s when the first athlete with a disability, Bob Hall, was integrated into the competitive field. At this time, this was innovative and groundbreaking; and importantly, it set the stage for inclusive practices for decades to come," said Paralympic champion Dr. Cheri Blauwet, BAA board chair. "Although these practices are now considered commonplace, it's important to remember that it all started at Boston."

Even the qualifying standards seemingly elevated Boston's status after they were first introduced in 1970; it has become a lore of attraction to BQ (Boston Qualify) in one's lifetime. In response to their concern that a field of no more than 1,000 is ideal to maintain the race's quality and course safety, the BAA stated in the 1970 race application, "A runner must submit the certification of either the Long Distance Running chairman of the Amateur Athletics Union of his district or his college coach that he has

Marathon Daffodils at the Boston Marathon Marker Memorial. *Photo by Paul Clerici.*

trained sufficiently to finish the course in less than four hours. This is not a jogging race."

BQ standards and processes have obviously changed, as has the field. In fact, the BAA received a record-setting 33,000 qualifying applications for the 2024 Boston, just over 2,500 more than the previous record from 2019.

"Receiving a record number of qualifier applications is a testament to the strength of road racing around the world and speaks to runners' commitment to taking on the challenge of earning a Boston Marathon qualifying time with the goal of reaching the start line in Hopkinton," said BAA CEO and president Jack Fleming.

Another unique aspect is the Boston Marathon Charity Program, which raised $6,600 via one charity when it began in 1989. It has, over the decades, expanded to more than 150 different officially accepted charities each year (participants bypass qualifying standards for entry by raising funds) and has raised over half a billion dollars.

And with greater sensitivity and the fact the Boston Marathon has fielded several Native American top finishers—William Davis, Mohawk (1901 runner-up); Thomas Longboat, Onondaga (1907 winner); U.S. Olympian Andrew Sockalexis, Penobscot (two-time runner-up); Russell George,

Onondaga (27th in 1939); Ellison "Deerfoot" Brown, Narragansett (two-time winner); Patti (Catalano) Dillon, Mi'kmaq (three-time runner-up)—the BAA has recognized its awareness with the following Indigenous and Native American Land Acknowledgment statement: "We run on the homelands of the Nipmuc and Massachusett. Long before the Boston Athletic Association was created, and still to this day, Indigenous and Native American people have run on these lands—their homeland. We acknowledge the trauma experienced over centuries by the Indigenous people who live on these lands and continue to face injustice. We honor with gratitude those peoples who have stewarded this land throughout the generations and their ongoing contributions to the region. We look forward to our continued collaboration in the years ahead. We thank all Indigenous and Native Americans who have shared and continue to share their stories."

This book will explore several of the longer-standing and more salient traditions and lore built on decades of history. While I have previously explored these subjects, to varying degrees, in *Marathon & Beyond*, *New England Runner*, and other newspapers, magazines, and books, in these pages they will be delved into deeper and with greater detail. Subjects include the Greece-made olive-branch champion wreaths; the colorfully painted start and finish lines and everything in between; the coveted unicorn-adorned finisher medals; the decades-long cultural and athletic relationship between the Boston Marathon and Japan's Ohme-Hochi 30K; the separate all-encompassing athlete villages for the elite and amateur participants; the ever-evolving media coverage; and the many on-the-course statues and monuments honoring the people and events of the race.

Each participant of any Boston Marathon—a one-timer or Quarter Century Club member (25 consecutive years or more); an overall champion or back-of-the-pack finisher; an age-group winner or charity runner—is infused with and connected to that long thread of history dating back to the late nineteenth century.

People don't just *run* the Boston Marathon—they become *part* of the Boston Marathon.

1

CHAMPION WREATHS FROM GREECE

One of the most recognizable symbols of athletic achievement is the wreath on a champion's head. It instantly signifies greatness.

The crowning of an olive-branch wreath atop the winner at the Boston Marathon is far from a cliché. There is a deep, soulful connection and meaning between the wreath, the Boston Marathon, the Olympics, and Greece. The history of that thread actually intertwines itself over thousands of years, and miles, to ancient Greek mythology. The bestowment by the Boston Athletic Association (BAA) is a great symbol of peace, competition, and unity.

The rich history of the ancient Olympic Games dates to at least 776 BC, as detailed in the International Olympic Committee's (IOC) *The Olympic Games of the Antiquity*. Myth and legend recount that Olympic Games predate humans via galactic competitions between such deities as Kronos (the King of Heaven) against Zeus (the Greek god of all gods), as noted in Aaron Atsma's *The Theoi Project: Greek Mythology*. For 1,170 years, until it fell victim to abolishment by conquering Roman emperor Theodosius I in AD 393—as a result of his converted religious stand against all things pagan—the Games were held in honor of Zeus in the shadows of his many monuments and temples in Olympia, Greece, according to *The Olympic Games of the Antiquity*.

During these approximate 292 quadrennial ancient Olympic Games that were held in Olympia every four years—a period of time known in Greek as an Olympiad—in each event, only one champion was announced and

Boston Marathon champion wreath in its natural state. *Photo by Paul Clerici.*

received a number of symbolic items of victory and at the conclusion of the Games was crowned with the lone official prize of an olive-branch wreath.

The sacred nature of the olive branch can be traced to nearly 1000 BC in Olympia, where olive trees were among the vegetation that grew in the religious land of Altis, where it is believed Zeus was widely worshiped, as explained in *The Olympic Games of the Antiquity*. It was in Altis, as noted in *The Theoi Project: Greek Mythology*, solely a place of worship, where legend tells the tale of two adult children of gods: Apollo (son of Zeus) and Daphne (daughter of Peneus), the latter of whom continually refused the relentless pursuit of the former. As a result of Apollo's derision toward Eros (aka Cupid) and his non-warrior use of a bow and arrow, by Eros a covert arrow of love was shot into Apollo and one of hate into Daphne, forever cursing Apollo to never receive Daphne's love. Apollo's incessant hunt finally forced Daphne—while fleeing from Apollo—to seek help and call on her father, who instantly transformed her into a laurel tree. Destined never to marry her, Apollo resigned himself to declare this tree sacred with great honor.

Later, the decision to fashion a wreath made from the sacred branches near the Temple of Zeus is said to have originated from the Oracle of Delphi on request from Iphitus, king of Elis, as noted in *The Olympic Games in Ancient Greece, Athens* by general supervisor Nicolaos Yalouris.

Also woven in this classical fabric is the 490 BC historically blended tale of a soldier-messenger by the name of Pheidippides, dispatched during battle from Marathon, Greece, on a two-day approximate 150-mile journey to Sparta (to seek additional military forces) and then later on an approximate 24-mile run to Athens (with news of the Athenian defeat of the Persians).

"To me," noted 26.2 Foundation president and former Boston Marathon race director Tim Kilduff, "the most important connection that marathoning has to Greece is in fact ancient Greece. In 490 BC [at] the Battle of Marathon, the Athenian Army had to go through a forced march to get back to [defend] Athens. Persians had been beaten back in Marathon and they were circling around on the sea and were going to come into Athens in a different direction. That forced march, I would argue, is the first marathon—490 BC! The Athenian defenders became known as Freedom Fighters."

It was from that battle in Marathon that the mythological folklore of Pheidippides and his fatally delivered message originated; the superior Persian Army was defeated by the smaller Athenian forces at the two-months-long battle during the Greco-Persian Wars, which lasted some five decades.

"The battle was essentially the spiritual start of the marathon run. That was really the birth. It's evolved since then—had to wait a long time before somebody came up with this long-distance run in 1896—but the fact of the matter is, it's a legitimate connection," said Kilduff. "And if you look at what was at stake at that point—which is all the more reason to connect governments—what was at stake was, essentially, in Athens they were developing the democratic form of government and that battle allowed that development to continue. When you're out training for a marathon, you don't think about this. But it's pretty powerful stuff."

Symeon Tegos, a career diplomat who in August 2022 became Consul General of Greece in Boston, is fully aware of the impact of remembering and honoring this historic and sacred past.

"I think it's very relevant in today's world [that] it's the values of democracy and freedom that was at stake that bright morning in Marathon. This victory," he said, "it was a victory that unite[d] us all, it was a victory of understanding the world and the concept of the world. But since then, of course, the development that reached the shores of this beautiful new world [of America]. And it should not be considered [a] given. The fight continues every day. I think this event does not just belong to Boston, like the marathon does not just belong to Greece—it belongs to all civilizations of the land. It is a world-class event."

After the passage of nearly 1,500 years without the Games, archaeological digs began to uncover some of these centuries-old ruins, according to *The Olympic Games of the Antiquity*. In 1892, historian and educator Pierre de Coubertin of France began his quest to resurrect the Olympic Games, which eventually led two years later to the founding of the IOC and in April 1896 the first Modern Olympic Games.

Much like de Coubertin was swept up in the Olympic ideals, so too was the nine-year-old BAA of the Games of the I Olympiad in Athens, Greece. BAA athletes who competed there not only excelled in many events, but they also brought back with them the same values and spirit that had earlier propelled the Frenchman, as well as the idea of the marathon footrace. As a direct result of the BAA's highly successful participation in the 1896 Olympic Games, the Boston Marathon was born in 1897. The BAA's Tom Burke—who marked the start of the first Boston Marathon, in Ashland, with a drag of his heel for the Pleasant Street start line and delivered his reported simplistic "Go!" command—had won a pair of events at the first Modern Olympic Games and was ceremoniously presented by King George I of Greece olive-tree branches (in place of wreaths) as part of the official recognition, as described in the *Official Report of the Games of the I Olympiad, Athens, 1896*.

The base of *The Spirit of the Marathon* statue in Hopkinton shows 1946 Boston Marathon winner Stylianos Kyriakides wearing the champion wreath. *Photo by Paul Clerici.*

For even more times than in the Olympic Games themselves, Boston has crowned its victors with a wreath. As explained by former IOC media relations manager Sandrine Tonge, it is neither mandated by the IOC nor directed in the Olympic Charter to present wreaths; individual Organizing Committees for the Olympic Games (OCOG) have featured olive-branch wreaths in only four Games since its resurrection: 1896 Athens (olive-tree branches), 1912 Stockholm, 1936 Berlin, and 2004 Athens.

At the 2004 Athens Olympic Games, both U.S. Olympians Meb Keflezighi (Marathon silver) and Deena Kastor (Marathon bronze) received one of those rare Olympic wreaths.

"Just prior to stepping into the stadium for the Olympic Marathon medal ceremony," Kastor recalled, "a presenter told us women that the six Marathon medalists—we three women and the three men who would compete a week later—will receive our laurel wreaths from Athena's ancient olive tree: 'It is a way of honoring an event with rich history here.' I was ecstatic!"

Seven days later, in the men's Marathon, the final event of the Games, Keflezighi was crowned in front of 70,000 people in Athens Olympic Stadium as part of the closing ceremonies.

"It was amazing. That's the reason I chose the marathon," he said of his fourth career 42K. "My chances of medaling were in the 10K versus the marathon. But in life there's no shortcut and I wanted to help with the resurgence of U.S. distance running. I decided to go with the Marathon because it was in Athens and it was the original course and it [medal/wreath ceremony] would be in the closing ceremonies. There's no guarantee of getting a medal, but I wanted to compete and hopefully bring a medal home and I wasn't going to be picky what medal it's going to be. There was a lot of history there. It was overwhelming."

Massachusetts native Shalane Flanagan, who won 10,000-meter silver at the 2008 Beijing Olympics, which did not include a wreath presentation, was nevertheless familiar with the Boston Marathon wreath history when she ran her home-state 26.2-miler in 2014. She held it in high enough regard as a lofty career goal.

"I have a good friend, Joan Benoit Samuelson, and for three years she'd told me to run my own race," said Flanagan, of the two-time Boston winner and 1984 U.S. Olympic Marathon gold medalist, at the 2014 Boston. "I wanted to go out and do just that. I wanted to see if it was good enough to win the olive wreath."

At the Boston Marathon, it has been a tradition reportedly since 1931. George Constantine Demeter, a university law professor and author of the parliamentary law book *Demeter's Manual of Parliamentary Law and Procedure*, was the first Greek American in the Massachusetts House of Representatives and had delivered to Boston from Greece the wreath made from Hellenic olive branches, the makeup of which differs from a laurel wreath comprised of bay laurel leaves and branches.

For 17 years (1931–47), Demeter cherished the honor of crowning the champions, one of whom was his sponsored pride and joy—from the Paphos village of Statos, Cyprus—1936 Greek Olympian Stylianos "Stelios" Kyriakides.

At the 1936 Berlin Olympics, in the presence of German chancellor and Nazi dictator Adolf Hitler, Kyriakides competed in the Marathon field that included U.S. Olympian Johnny "The Elder" Kelley, 1935 Boston champion. The two athletes became friends, and the Cyprus native two years later ran the 1938 Boston. Among the spectators along the Boston course was future governor of Massachusetts Michael Dukakis, a four-year-old first-generation Greek American from Brookline, Massachusetts, whose longtime connection to the race and its heritage was just beginning.

"Pheidippides' run—running from Marathon to Athens to tell the Greeks that we had beaten the Persians—every Greek kid knew that story," noted Dukakis. "First [Boston] Marathon I watched was in 1938 [when Kyriakides] dropped out. It was terrible; the Greeks were [all disappointed]."

Eight years later, at the 1946 Boston, Kyriakides returned to compete against Kelley, his friend and defending champion. On the Greek's shoulders stood more than personal pride. Kyriakides carried with him the hopes of his post–World War II homeland, which was destroyed by the Nazis, whose Schutzstaffel (SS) soldiers nearly killed him during the war.

"In retaliation [of the Greek Resistance fighters], to try to terrorize the civilian population, the Nazis, on a Sunday, would kind of swoop into a particular part of Athens, send the women and kids home, round up all the men, and hang them so that people going to work on Monday morning would see these guys hanged," Dukakis explained. "Kyriakides was one of the folks who was caught up in this thing; he was just out with his family on a Sunday. So this Nazi officer told him to empty his pockets and he has his identification card from the '36 Olympics, which might have even had Hitler's picture on it or [a Swastika]. The officer looks at it [and tells Kyriakides to] 'Pick up your stuff and go home.' He had almost been executed by the Nazis during World War II."

By the time Kyriakides arrived for the 1946 Boston, he was so underweight that his journey nearly ended before it began.

"He didn't weigh 120 pounds—his wife thought he was nuts, everybody thought he was nuts [to run]," said Dukakis. "The doctors in Hopkinton turned him down—they wouldn't let him run. George Demeter vouched for him."

At the Hotel Minerva he owned in Boston, Demeter had housed and fed the 36-year-old Greek. And on Patriots' Day, by a full two minutes, Kyriakides (2:29:27) battled Kelley (2:31:27) to victory in the fifth-fastest time over the first 20 years Boston was 42 kilometers. From the sidelines, a 12-year-old Dukakis personally witnessed this momentous race.

"I was there in Kenmore Square when Kyriakides and Kelley were running neck and neck in 1946," Dukakis recalled. "In those days, no television, no transistor radios, no nothing—you didn't know [about the leaders] until you heard the state troopers on their motorcycles coming down [the street]. Word starts coming down it's Kelley and the Greek! As they came down Kenmore Square, Kyriakides began moving out ahead of Johnny Kelley. Of course us Greek kids were terribly conflicted because we loved Kelley, but this [Kyriakides] guy was Greek! It was an incredible race. He stuck around the United States—the Greeks were starving at the time because it was after World War II—and he brought back millions of dollars worth of relief supplies. He became a national hero."

At the 1951 Boston, Dukakis as a 17-year-old student ran in a time of 3:31:00 for 57th place, 10 spots ahead of seven-time champion Clarence DeMar. Then, 24 years later—37 years after he watched his first Boston Marathon—Dukakis further deepened his relationship with the race when he was elected the 65th governor of Massachusetts. As such, one of his first duties found him three months later at the finish-line podium stage to present the medal and wreath on Patriots' Day, April 21, 1975, when Greater Boston Track Club's Bill Rodgers won the first of his four titles.

"I always aimed hard for the win at Boston," said Rodgers, "and it was always a tremendous feeling of satisfaction and happiness when I did win and received the unique gold medal and laurel wreath."

Dukakis is proud of his national heritage and multipronged connection to the Boston Marathon, as the first Massachusetts—and second U.S.—Greek American governor, longest tenured governor in office (12 years), 1988 Democratic nominee for the presidency of the United States, and Boston Marathon podium presenter.

"I got elected in the Legislature in '62," he said. "It was inconceivable at that time a Greek American could be elected governor of Massachusetts. Not because people didn't like us, it was just the ethnic politics of the state;

Four-time Boston Marathon winner Bill Rodgers and his wreath from 1975. *Photo by Paul Clerici.*

look how long it took before we had an Italian American mayor of the City of Boston!"

Dukakis has always recognized the importance of the Boston Marathon to the Greek community, as well as to his Massachusetts hometown, which hosts 2.25 miles of the course.

"Remember, for Brookline kids, this was the event. We were all out there. [And] when I was a kid, I don't remember the governor being a presence [at the podium presentation]; it was always the mayor," he said. "They knew I had run and I was obviously going to be there [as governor]. Whether they decided at that point that it might be a good idea for the governor with my connection—I wanted to be there. When I became governor, to be able to be up there in some fashion [was special]."

The tradition of the wreaths nearly disappeared in the early 1980s when the Boston Marathon was dealing with layers of destructive turmoil, public apathy, the Rosie Ruiz cheating scandal, and multiple warring

Massachusetts governor Michael Dukakis holds a photograph of himself when he crowned 1986 Boston Marathon winner Rob de Castella with the wreath. *Photo by Paul Clerici.*

factions surrounding the race. It was also a time that included the very real possibility of losing the event when a potential deal had apparently turned over control to a Boston lawyer (while the BAA would still organize the race). Lawsuits and bad press followed. And this was all under the constant watchful eyes of the many television news stations, radio stations, and major newspapers.

"It was bad. Everybody was mad at us," recalled Kilduff, race director from 1983 to 1984 after he replaced Will Cloney, who served as the first race director, from 1947 to 1982. (Previously, the race was organized by committee.) "The runners were mad at us; there was the whole amateur-versus-professional thing where [the BAA] wasn't going to pay [prize] money;

we had to straddle a number of demands and needs. And the overriding issue was the court case. And don't forget the environment in which we were operating—we were running on instinct then. Nobody managed this then. There were no files when Will Cloney left. It was all disjointed. And at the press conferences, they'd all show up! The Boston Marathon then was a 12-month-a-year story."

Guy Morse III, the Boston Marathon's third race director (1985–2000), whose first experience with the race was as a Prudential Insurance employee who as a race volunteer was in charge of finish-line and media room activities, recalls that the early 1980s were indeed difficult times.

"My first recollection was one of some stress," he remembered. "Probably around 1981 or 1982, I recall having to come up with a 'Plan B,' as there was a chance the official wreaths would not arrive in time from Greece. At that time, many things seemed very loosely organized and as the race itself was going through so much turmoil, a detail like the wreaths was left to chance. In any event, I secured 'back-up wreaths' made and stored by a local florist, which I believe we actually had to use one of those years."

Around the time the Massachusetts Supreme Judicial Court eventually ruled to void the contract deal—which returned the Boston Marathon to the BAA, after nearly four years in the courts—in 1984, there arose a literal olive branch of peace from the very heart of its origin. Greek American *Hellenic Chronicle* newspaper publisher and editor Peter Agris of Boston proposed the idea of formally bridging a direct link between the Boston Marathon and Greece by way of perpetual olive-branch wreaths direct from the Hellenic Republic. *The Hellenic Chronicle* Digitation Project executive director Nancy Agris Savage, also a former editor-in-chief of *The Hellenic Chronicle*, knew of her late father's strong Greek pride and determination and was not surprised at his idea.

"The offices of *The Hellenic Chronicles* were at the corner of Newbury and Hereford Streets, where we had a front-row seat as the winners turned the corner of their last leg of the 26.2-mile journey," she recalled. "I think it was his favorite day of the year. But something was missing—the piece where runners and spectators alike actually got why anyone would undertake a grueling road race of this nature in the first place. It was this passion to remind us all of every instance where Greek history had left a mark on modern civilization that led him in the spring of 1984 to reach out [to local leaders]."

One of those individuals was Kilduff, who instantly recognized the importance of this connection.

"I didn't know him," Kilduff said of Agris. "He was—the word is philhellene—a promoter of Greece, a student of Greece. He saw the opportunity and the pride. He was a big representative of the Greek Americans. A very sincere guy. So when he called, it was totally instinctive. It sounded like the right thing to do. He wanted those wreaths to be assembled, put together, and shipped here [to Boston from Greece]. It was a no-brainer! He had his heart in the right place."

Kilduff brought the proposal to the BAA Board of Governors, where a brief discussion took place concerning the process and the details. In a letter to the office of then–Boston mayor Raymond Flynn, dated 11 days prior to the 1984 Boston Marathon, Agris confirmed the details, stating in part: "Beginning with the 1984 BAA Marathon on April 16, the Government of Greece will…arrange each year to send two olive wreaths and two medals direct from the birthplace of the Marathon in Greece.… On the day of the Marathon, April 16, Mayor Flynn and Gov. Dukakis will place the authentic wreaths on the heads of the male and female victors at the finish line."

Then–Consul General of Greece in Boston Christos Panagopoulos, in a letter that same week to Mayor Flynn, stated, in part, "It is of significance that the wreaths and medals are similar to those which were presented to the winners in ancient Greece, where the Marathon and Olympic Games originated. Needless to say, my dear Mayor Flynn, if these presentations contribute to the success of this outstanding event, my Government will be gratified to provide the wreaths and medals annually."

Kilduff and Morse, Boston race directors during this transition period, both understood the significance of this new venture.

"It's a gift," acknowledged Kilduff. "The concept of a gift from the people of Greece is how this all started. You know, I have a decent understanding of the marathon from a logistical, technical, and organizational perspective, but it wasn't until I visited Marathon, Greece, and stood on the ground near the Tomb of the Athenians that I got the historic and emotional connection. Every year, I sit there with a big smile on my face [seeing] this once simple ceremony now being such a big platform for telling this story of the marathon, ancient Greece, Stylianos Kyriakides, and the Battle of Marathon."

The Alpha Omega Council—the Greek-American men's organization Agris founded in 1976 to help spread Hellenic awareness—is also involved in promoting this message. Nicholas Kourtis, 26.2 Foundation director and Marathon Education Committee chairman and an Alpha Omega Council

Consul General of Greece in Boston Symeon Tegos (*far left at podium*) at the 2023 wreath ceremony in the Consulate General of Greece in Boston function room. *Photo by Paul Clerici.*

past president, fully embraced that connection, especially as a tool for people to learn more about that lineage.

"[That Greek victory over the Persians] allowed ancient Greek civilization to flourish and make advances in democracy, science, philosophy, and the arts, all of which have provided the basis of much of Western Civilization as we now know it," Kourtis pointed out. "It has also inspired others to stand against powerful empires and improbable odds in the defense of liberty. [The Patriots' Day link] is the embodiment of the citizen-solder concept running from ancient Athens to Lexington-Concord and their Minutemen also facing down an empire in defense of republican liberty."

While inherently rich in history, the Boston Marathon and those wreaths are a bond that Morse sees as intrinsic.

"In the case of the Boston winners' olive wreaths, to me, it was of utmost importance to resurrect and nurture that tradition in particular. So many other traditions and usual ways of doing business were being tested and often abandoned in the name of progress," he said. "The wreaths, I realized, were not only a sacred link to our past, but in actuality were linked to our very birth. Additionally, the wreaths and the relationship with Greece also symbolized the importance and worldwide support this Marathon enjoyed. Such support and celebration should not be taken for granted or given less than our full attention, no matter how complex the event otherwise becomes. As such, and as time-tested, the Boston wreaths may be the single most enduring symbol of success, endurance, and grace in our or any sport."

Peter Lemonias, Alpha Omega Council past president, who also chaired the 2014 and 2015 Boston Marathon wreath ceremonies, endeavored to continue that which the founder began.

"The wreath ceremony helps remind all [of us] of the Boston Marathon's Greek origins," he noted. "The wreaths presented at the wreath ceremony are a gift of Greece and her people to the BAA and all the people associated with the Marathon."

Those early days of the renewed collaboration were simpler compared to its current grandeur.

"Of note," Morse pointed out, "when you look at some of the early photos—for example, Johnny Kelley's wins—the wreathes are made of laurel, and I believe we moved to the more authentic crown of olive branches when we formalized our relationship and support of the country of Greece and the local Greek community."

Explained Agris Savage, "Flown from Athens via Olympic Airways, the crudely fashioned wreaths resembled the original crowns presented to the Olympic Games victors with the symbolic olive branches, ancient symbols of peace. Beginning in 1984, they were presented by Greek Consulate of Boston officials to BAA officials at a special ceremony at the Consulate offices several days before the running of the Boston Marathon."

The first winners to be crowned by this new official tradition were Geoff Smith of Great Britain and Lorraine Moller of New Zealand, both of whom won Boston in the Olympic year of 1984.

"It was all about qualifying for the Olympics that year, so I really didn't know about the wreath till I finished the race," noted Smith. "Winning the race was fantastic, having the medal put over me [head] was even better; the wreath was something special."

After the post-Demeter years of other dignitaries presenting the wreath, such as Boston fire commissioner Thomas Grifin in the 1960s, it became customary for the city's leader to place the wreath. Oftentimes during Mayor Flynn's administration, however, he was usually a runner instead of a presenter, so in those instances the first lady of Boston, Catherine Flynn, performed the honor.

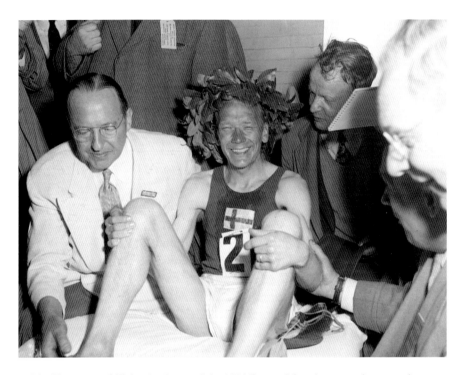

Veikko Karvonen of Finland, winner of the 1954 Boston Marathon, wearing an early version of the wreath. *Courtesy of the Boston Public Library, Leslie Jones Collection.*

"Yeah, the mayor was running, so it was put on by his wife. She put it on and the wreath fell over me head! It was big!" recalled Smith with a laugh. "But I was in college! I was a single guy. Back then, you didn't stay in hotels, there was no prize money. I stayed with a family out in Holliston—Barry and Sandy Sims—and I gave them the wreath as a thank-you. And they've had it preserved in a display box."

Smith did likewise in 1985, when he defended his title and again gave his wreath to the Sims family.

"If I had kept it, it would have been destroyed," he noted. "They did a fantastic job with them."

Moller, who four months later came in fifth in the first Olympic Women's Marathon, at the 1984 Los Angeles Games, and then won Marathon bronze at the 1992 Barcelona Games, recognizes the relevance of the treasured honor.

"I was delighted with the connection between Boston and Greece via the wreaths," she said. "The visions of ancient Olympics added to the allure and mystique that Boston Marathon already held for me. Winning is always its own brand of high. Boston Marathon is at the top of this list. When the wreath was placed on my head, I was not just the winner, but the 'Queen of Boston' for that day. So proud!"

Moller also was generous enough to lend her wreath to Gloria Ratti, the late BAA vice president and secretary of the board of governors, who collected and curated Boston Marathon–related items to preserve its history.

"The wreath is currently on loan to the Boston Marathon museum, along with [my] medal. I loaned them to Gloria for the opening and she was a little fierce about giving them back. God bless her! I do miss her!!" said Moller. "Sometime soon I'd like to retrieve them. Boston Marathon remains first place in my heart amongst marathons."

The related ceremonies have grown over the years. Early finish-line presentations consisted of only the exuberance of a lone official—usually Demeter in full suit, jacket, and tie—chasing after the winner at the finish line in an attempt to immediately place the wreath on the new champion's head in a somewhat "dignified" manner. There were times, however, when he waited for the moment the winner did actually stop. VIPs soon joined the festivities, as well as the fixture of some kind of staging. In 1968, when Ambrose "Amby" Burfoot of Wesleyan University won, however, he was more concerned about remaining upright.

"I remember my complete collapse into [race official John] 'Jock' Semple's strong arms. I felt like an overcooked noodle at that point—a fairly apt description, given the warm sun and temperatures of the day," Burfoot recalled. "After that, it's all a blur."

Semple held up the senior All-American long enough for the champ to make his way to the temporary stage on Ring Road, where Boston mayor Kevin White placed the wreath.

"I remember that the laurel wreath was too large, so it seemed to slip down onto my ears," Burfoot said. "Other than that, there were a lot of dignitaries around and a lot of people holding my arm up in the air—I probably needed their help—and I was up on some kind of platform looking down at big crowds."

Rodgers won Boston four times between 1975 and 1980, and while the award presentation was nevertheless noteworthy enough to be accompanied by race officials, politicians, media, and spectators, the finish-line pomp was still in its infancy.

"The Boston Marathon was not so tightly choreographed as it is now, [and] that includes the finish line for the winners," he pointed out. "There was no national anthem played; however, each instance I was quickly

Massachusetts state representative George Constantine Demeter *(far right)* with a wreath from Greece, about to crown Stylianos Kyriakides for winning in 1946. *Courtesy of the Boston Public Library, Leslie Jones Collection.*

gathered up by several policemen and taken to a sort-of podium where the laurel wreath was placed on my head."

In the ensuing years, though, while winners were still being crowned at the Boston Marathon, the reverence began to fade, recalled Kilduff. Enter Constantinos Orphanides, the Consul General of Greece in Boston at that time. To coincide with the 2006 unveiling in Hopkinton of *The Spirit of the Marathon* statue of Kyriakides and 1896 Athens Olympic Marathon winner Spiridon Louis, a formal wreath-receiving ceremony was instituted inside the Consulate General of Greece in Boston building.

"The [wreath] order went to Greece in plenty of time for creation and transport of the wreaths—on Olympic Airways most of the time—and at no cost to the BAA or the City," said Morse. "The consul general for many years stored the wreaths in a refrigeration unit at the Consulate and delivered them to us on race day. In later years, we formalized the presentation of the wreaths to the BAA in a more appropriate ceremony that the special relationship deserved, and thereby had all the important items in our hands several days prior to the event. They were kept cold and 'spritzed,' first at our florist's locations, then at our own offices on race weekend."

The actual boughs from which the wreaths would be fashioned originated from olive trees grown around the Tomb of the Athenians, sacred land in Athens, Greece, where soldiers from the 490 Battle of Marathon are entombed.

"In the past, the wreaths have been cut from olive trees in the beautiful areas of Greece around ancient Marathon, carefully woven into wreaths, and then sent to the United States and to Boston via the secure auspices of the Greek Foreign Ministry," noted Kourtis.

That bond has resonated with Kilduff due to his many visits to the hallowed grounds.

"The olive branches that make up the olive wreaths…are from olive trees in Marathon, Greece, that surround the Tomb of the Athenians where the Athenian soldiers, who gave their lives defending democracy against the Persians, are buried. That's the emotional connection," he noted. "There are significant commitments that people make in terms of running the marathon. But if you don't quite understand [the connection], it gets juiced up, it gets hyper-charged when you're on the ground, looking at the Tomb of the Athenians and realizing the connection and how that's come forward. That to me is the exciting part."

It cannot be emphasized enough the significance of not only the location from where the wreath originates but also the visceral connection to life as it is known today.

"We always have to remember it was this civilization that also start thinking in terms of human being at the center of the universe. We Greeks put the human being at the center of the universe. Not just us [Greeks, but all human beings]," said Tegos. "At the same time, touching it, seeing it —it gets you there. This connection that the Americans have with Greece, not only the values but actually they go to Marathon, to Olympia, to the Thessaloniki, to all those beautiful ancient places that are still there and you can see where everything started."

Tegos was filled with national pride on learning the history of the Boston Marathon wreaths, especially its 1984 resurgence powered by his Consulate General of Greece in Boston and the Alpha Omega Council in Boston. It was even more meaningful to him that the wreaths are still made of branches from olive trees that surround the Tomb of Marathon.

"I'm very honored and humbled," he noted. "It's the values that it represents. The cities back in the day fought for a certain purpose and a

At the Massachusetts State House Great Hall, *from left*: Consul General of Greece in Boston Stratos Efthymiou, BAA Board of Governor president Dr. Michael O'Leary, Boston mayor Marty Walsh, and Alpha Omega Council event chairman John Kopellas, in 2019. *Photo by Paul Clerici.*

connection between the [original] run and the marathon. From the ancient time to the modern time, it's evident it connects our values. So democracy, human dignity, freedom—all that we stand, even now as a world—started back then with this run [in 490 BC]. And with [Pheidippides's apocryphal] last words 'nenikekiam'—which means 'We won!'—it's not just a win for the Athenians back then, but it was a win also for the concept of the world as we know it today."

It was largely due to the increase in communication, organization, and planning that the foresight from the Greek community and the BAA put together a worthy ceremony of the wreaths' arrival and delivery.

"It's evolved," said Kilduff of the wreaths, presentations, and ceremonies. "To drive home the connection to ancient Greece, that's what motivates all of this. People run marathons all over the world. Do they understand its origins? Most of them probably don't. The Hellenic community got involved, the BAA, the Greek American community, Alpha Omega Council,

Dimitri [Kyriakides] with the Stylianos Kyriakides story and statue, and in 2010 the 2500th anniversary of the Battle of Marathon—it all fits in. All parts of the evolution."

That evolution has grown from the wreath being delivered by hand at the airport decades ago to full pageantry at the Massachusetts State House or the Consulate General of Greece in Boston building. The Consul General of Greece in Boston receives the wreaths from their homeland and in front of various dignitaries presents them to the BAA.

"In addition to remarks of the consul general and the BAA executives, we typically have the singing of the national anthems of Greece and USA, remarks by Metropolitan Methodios of the Greek Orthodox Church, remarks by political leaders, and others," Lemonias detailed. "The audience consists of political leaders, interested academics, athletic directors, Marathon-related organization representatives, Marathon runners, former star runners of the Boston Marathon, members of the Boston diplomatic community, and representatives of numerous Greek-American organizations."

In honor of the 2500th anniversary of the Battle of Marathon, for the first time, gold-dipped olive-branch wreaths were awarded to the winners

Wreath ceremony at the Great Hall inside the Massachusetts State House. *Photo by Paul Clerici.*

of the 2010 Boston. That special connection between Greece and Boston was also heightened and strengthened in the aftermath of the bombings that shattered the 2013 Boston Marathon. In recognition of Boston Strong and all that carried the community, Boston, and the world to the first-anniversary 2014 race, gold-dipped olive-branch wreaths from Greece were once again created.

The 2014 gilded bestowals were presented by then–Consul General of Greece in Boston Iphigenia Karas to then-BAA president Joann Flaminio in a ceremony held at the Great Hall inside the Massachusetts State House. And on race day, 2014 winners Ernst Van Dyk (men's wheelchair), Tatyana McFadden (women's wheelchair), Rita Jeptoo (women's open), and Keflezighi (men's open), were respectively crowned by BAA Board of Governors vice president Dr. John Coyle, BAA Board of Governor Dr. Michael O'Leary, Massachusetts governor Deval Patrick, and Boston mayor Marty Walsh.

Boston Marathon gold-dipped olive-branch champion wreath. *Photo by Paul Clerici.*

"It has truly been a personal honor to place the wreath on the winner's head," Dr. Coyle recognized. "And every time, I am struck by its significance going back to the original ancient Olympic Marathons, where the winner received the wreath as his prize. To be affiliated with such an important legacy is awe-inspiring. [It] is a permanent representation and signifies the long-standing and lasting association the BAA has with Greece and the historic context of the birthplace of all marathons."

The first American to receive the golden wreath, in 2014, was McFadden, the adopted Russian-born defending champion Paralympian from Illinois. As a member of Team MR8—named in honor of Martin W. Richard, the youngest of the fatal bombing victims—she wore the ubiquitous Team MR8 yellow and blue jersey as she set a 10-minute personal record.

"When the race is done, you get some water really quickly, answer a few questions, and then do the ceremony where you get the medal, hold the trophy, and then they put the wreath on my head," she said. "[The wreath] was definitely beautiful, absolutely gorgeous. [In 2013] it was a different kind of wreath, but [the gold-dipped wreath] reminded me of Athens, very goddess-like. It was heavy for a wreath, but it was amazing putting that on. It was just a gorgeous, gorgeous, gorgeous wreath!"

Immediately following the ceremony, McFadden—as the champions often do—continued the celebration and appreciation by saluting the spectators along the nearby bleacher sections on Boylston Street. She noticed in the stands the big cowboy hat atop Carlos Arredondo, the spectator–turned–first responder in 2013 who was captured in an iconic image as he aided severely injured survivor Jeff Bauman out of harm's way.

"The cowboy," McFadden said with a smile. "I really wanted to give the wreath to him. Just reading his story, knowing his background. He gave so much support to Boston and being so brave—everyone being so brave—I really wanted to give him the wreath on behalf of everyone as a thank-you. When I saw him, that's when the thought went into my head. At that moment."

Dr. O'Leary is also well aware of the significance of the prep and presentation.

"A member of the BAA staff prepares the champions trophy, medallions, and olive wreaths for presentation. All who have the responsibility understand the importance of the moment and the achievement, and so the presentations are conducted with reverence fitting the ceremony," said the former BAA board chair.

Eritrean-born U.S. citizen Keflezighi punctuated the emotional and cathartic vibe in Boston when he became the first American men's winner since Greg Meyer's victory in 1983. Keflezighi's heartfelt exuberance and pride was seen and felt worldwide when he blessed himself and then punched the air in excitement as he crossed the hallowed finish line in 2014.

Keflezighi—who was initially unaware that the 2014 edition of the olive wreath was dipped in gold, as he had previously seen its natural green predecessors on several occasions—has grown to appreciate the selfless commitment Stylianos Kyriakides exhibited decades earlier and has met his son, Dimitri Kyriakides, who maintains that vigil to keep his father's benevolence and honor alive.

"I didn't know that right away, but it was [in] one of the 9,000 e-mails that I got," Keflezighi said with a laugh in reference to a correspondence from Dimitri Kyriakides after the 2014 Boston win. "He did send me that [info] about the wreath and the similarities between his dad and myself. [We'd talked about] his inspiring father and what he's done after he won the Boston Marathon. I didn't know that," he noted, and then added about the wreaths, "I knew they came from Greece. And then to have it and then [for it] to come now, full circle, to not only get the wreath of olive leaves that come from the actual olive trees surrounding the fallen Athenians at the tomb which I ran [past on] the course in 2004 in the Olympic Games—and in 24k gold—it's amazing!"

American Paralympic gold and silver medalist Susannah Scaroni, who was the 2022 Boston runner-up, won the following year and cherishes her crown.

"I was told (in 2022) that they came from Greece and I had never, ever been aware of that," she said, "and so I honestly forgot about the wreath until it was placed on my head and it all came back to me just how special a thing it is that they are transported here from Greece. I didn't know anything else about the symbolism of those particular (connections) themselves, which to me now, is just so special. It's those small things that races like Boston are so iconic for because they make every moment as special as they can be, which makes a win here as special as it can be because the best of the best are here because of all those small things coming together. It's an honor to wear that. It's my favorite thing for sure! I have a gold medal I earned at the Tokyo Paralympics and next to that is this gold wreath. Honestly, that's really special."

Six-time Boston winner and Switzerland Paralympic gold (6), silver (4), and bronze (2) medalist Marcel Hug, who has received champion wreaths at other marathons—Berlin and New York, for instance—was initially unaware of its historic connection between Boston and Greece.

"I didn't know the story about Greece and now it's even nicer to know. It really belongs to Boston," he marveled. "It's a great symbol and it's such a great honor to receive the wreath from Greece. It belongs to the Boston Marathon, so it's very special."

That awareness, or lack thereof, in some instances, is part of the reason behind the constant effort to keep the story alive, especially for BAA CEO and president Jack Fleming.

"It's interesting sometimes to watch different sports, even our sport, and they may present or crown a champion with a wreath of leaves and it sort of [just] happens. And I wonder whether they know why they are doing it," he observed. "There's definitely a ceremonial aspect, yes, but you hear, even in audio, sometimes incorrectly referred to—well, maybe it is depending upon what they are using (laurel leaves)—as the laurel wreath. It's a symbol of victory, but here at Boston, when we see the olive wreath, it brings us back to our roots. For us, the authentic connection is with the 1896 Modern Olympic Games in Athens and when many members of the BAA team members comprised some of the U.S. Olympic team. I just hope that it's something that, if anybody else does it, that they do it with intention and meaning and with respect and knowing the story. It can have value in many different ways, but with respect is how we would like to see these things regarded just because it is part of our heritage, too."

For both the presenter and the receiver, the placing of the wreath comes with it the historical lineage of those who have come before, from mythical gods and heads of state to the greatest specimens and elite athletes.

"That the olive wreaths have arrived from Greece is lost on no one involved with the BAA," said Dr. O'Leary. "We understand our historical roots and we are proud of continuing our traditions for all to witness in this very public ceremony. Certainly, the presentation of the olive wreaths to the champions is one of the most visible and direct ties to our past and communicates instantly to a worldwide audience our heritage."

Kastor noted of her knowledge prior to her first wreath, "I was an English major with emphasis in creative writing and a second major in journalism, so I knew a lot about Greek literature. Add my love of the marathon and you can see that my love of the laurel wreath goes beyond signifying a win. It signifies rich tradition, excellence, and honoring a history [of] great athletic achievement."

One aspect associated with the wreath that may not be thoroughly thought out at the time of receipt is how to safely bring it home. Due to its inherent delicate and fragile nature, it does take some planning.

"It is fragile because it is dipped in gold and it has a little weight to it," noticed Keflezighi of his 2014 crown. "A few [leaves] have come off, but at the same time, it is very delicate."

In Kastor's case, the 7,000-mile journey from the 2004 Athens Olympic Games all came down to the final hurdle at U.S. Customs and Border Protection inside Los Angeles International Airport.

"I hand-carried the wreath on the three airplane rides back to Los Angeles, but immigration said I couldn't bring it through customs because it was vegetation. 'Oh, no!' I begged, with no sign of the officer budging," Kastor recalled. "One of my teammates said, 'She just won a medal in the Olympics.' That is when my fate changed. In Olympic Team circles it's called dropping the 'O' word for the sake of benefits. The 'O' had been dropped, and after posing for photos with the officers wearing my medal, I was allowed to go through customs with my wreath in hand."

From the same Olympic Games, however, Keflezighi experienced a different fate when his wreath was reportedly stolen during the postrace press conference (a gold-dipped wreath was later mailed to him as a replacement). But after his 2014 Boston win, the wreath remained close to Keflezighi.

"We held onto it," he noted. "While I was doing my [post-Boston press] tours, my wife brought it home and packaged it."

The life of a wreath—natural or gold-dipped—can vary. It can wilt easily or live on in view inside a frame. Rodgers openly displayed his 1975 crown in a shadowbox at his Bill Rodgers Running Center store in Faneuil Hall Marketplace in Boston for nearly 35 years until the store closed in 2012.

"Charlie has my '75 laurel wreath," he said of his brother, who is now the keeper of the store's running memorabilia. "Neither of us knows what happened to the others. In '75, I [also] won a unique trophy that disappeared at some point after the laurel wreath and medal and trophy were presented to me. The trophy was in honor of being the first American runner that day as we celebrated our country's birthday. I never saw it again."

Kastor undertook a tremendous effort to protect, preserve, and display her Olympic treasure.

"The wreath hangs in a corner of our home's great room," she stated. "I had Joel St. Marie, a professional framer and photographer, treat the wreath with a preservative then create a shadowbox for it."

Smith's benevolence in 1984 and 1985 indirectly saved the life of his two wreaths. But Burfoot, however, has no recollection of the whereabouts of his.

"Gosh, I have no idea what became of the wreath," he wondered. "It might have gone back to Wesleyan with me or back to Groton [Connecticut] with my father. I never saved it or anything. I had a little winner's medal that said BAA Boston Marathon with a tiny diamond in it. And my memories. That was all I wanted."

Conversely, 1973 Boston winner Jacqueline Hansen preserved her wreath and 40 years later presented it to the BAA.

"Jacqueline Hansen came over to the office with a small package and she said, 'Oh, I've been thinking about this. I want you to have something.' It was her 1973 champion's olive wreath!" said Fleming. "She also gave her 1973 bib number to us, 1973 certificate of completion. The bib is great, the finisher's certificate is awesome, but the wreath and the way it's packaged (so well) really blew us away. To me, the olive wreath does conjure up our roots. That is how the marathon was founded, not the BAA, but the marathon! I love the fact that our champion and course-record medallions even include the olive wreath."

When the now gold-dipped wreaths are presented to the BAA—at the Massachusetts State House or inside the Consulate General of Greece in Boston building—that ceremony marks not only recognition for the future champions but also those who fought in Greece in 490 BC.

"Democracy, freedom—it was not just a city that they were defending back then," Tegos noted of the Athenians, "it was the whole concept and idea and relationship with the world. It all started then and that's why marathon has this symbolic value and also there is this concept that comes from that time to today. I have to tell you, I think this now belongs also to humanity. That's why you have a Boston Marathon, a Tokyo Marathon—it started [in Greece], but now it's something that belongs to all of us. It belongs to humanity, as a constant, as a way of life. We have to remember that. Today, it's much more global than when it just started."

Massachusetts governor Maura Healey, who in 2023 at her first Boston Marathon as head of the state presented the wreath to men's winner Evans Chebet, was filled with the legacy of the ceremony.

"It's incredibly meaningful and the symbolism of the wreath is something! The Boston Marathon is this iconic part of our history in Boston and in Massachusetts, and we take great pride in that. As governor, it was a tremendous honor and privilege to be able to place the wreath on the winner. It's a beautiful continuation that reflects back of course to the Olympics and that incredible achievement, and it's wonderful to see that memorialized and held up in the form of the Marathon today," she observed. "And if you go back to the Battle of Marathon, you think about the fight for democracy. We're proud here in Massachusetts where we're home to the world's oldest

Massachusetts governor Maura Healey places the wreath on 2023 Boston Marathon winner Evans Chebet of Kenya. *Photo by Paul Clerici.*

living written Constitution which became, really, the model for the United States Constitution; and so, we also celebrate Patriots' Day Weekend here in Boston and in Massachusetts and that's really significant. There's always work to do in keeping up our democracy, that's for sure. But as governor, I'm privileged to be able to be in a position to hopefully further that support in a civic engagement all around."

From galactic battles between gods to ancient Greek mythology to the Battle of Marathon and diplomatic exchanges between Greece and Boston, Kilduff hopes that the long-connected message of its history is not lost on new generations.

"Take that element now and you push it all the way through to modern day, it's exactly the concept that needs to be promoted now," he said. "That's the contribution that marathoning makes to the world. It's an expression of, yes, every marathoner has to make a personal decision to commit; it's a statement about personal freedom; and it's also, most importantly, an expression of the power of the human spirit. That's what the wreath symbolizes—it's that simple, it's the power of the human spirit. Current-day marathoners sometimes don't spend the time thinking about the historic significance of the history, but if these wreaths can help do that then the people of Greece had made a contribution to bringing that story forward. That's what presenting the wreaths to the Boston Marathon is all about."

Added Massachusetts Senate president Karen Spilka, whose district includes the first four communities of the Boston Marathon course—Hopkinton, Ashland, Framingham, and Natick, "At its heart, the Marathon is a celebration of endurance and persistence and sticking with it through really tough times. It's the celebration of the human spirit; it's as simple and as complex an event as that. It also brings together people from all over the world."

2

START LINE, FINISH LINE,
AND EVERYTHING BETWEEN

Two main goals for every Boston Marathon participant have remained the same each year since 1897: to reach the start line and the finish line. While the physical locations of each mark have changed a few times, everyone trains to reach the start line and then trusts that training to carry them to the finish line.

From 1897 to 1923, the race started in Ashland at three different locations over the first 27 years. In 1897 and 1898, it started on Pleasant Street, along the Boston and Albany Railroad tracks, near Metcalf's Mill at the Sudbury River. For the next eight years, from 1899 to 1906, the start line was located about .3 miles west of the first spot, on the High Street bridge over the railroad tracks. And for 17 years, from 1907 to 1923, the start was in the area of Valentine farm, on Hopkinton Road at Steven's Corner, near the current 4K (2.48 miles) mark on West Union Street/Route 135.

When 15 men toed that first start line, it had been dug in the road by U.S. Olympic medalist Tom Burke, of race organizer Boston Athletic Association (BAA), who simply dragged his heel across Pleasant just prior to the 12:19 p.m. start when he reportedly exclaimed the equally simple command of "Go!"

For decades, the start and finish lines were usually a single white line painted on the course—sometimes no start line when the ground was muddy; and occasionally the finish line included a few words of its location—and the course featured minimal structural support or design elements.

Later, in the shadow of Hopkinton Town Common and Marathon Way, the start area features more than 1,200 barricades and fencing for the corrals,

Top: Stage-high view of the start line of the Boston Marathon. *Photo by Jennifer Edwards.*

Bottom: A single white line marked the finish of the 1966 Boston Marathon on Ring Road. *Courtesy City of Boston.*

Not even a discernable start line can be seen in the mud of the 1912 Boston Marathon in Ashland. *Courtesy the Sports Museum of New England/Ashland Historical Society.*

security areas, crowd control, and to line the beginning of the race. Between the start line and the northeast corner of the common is located a large fenced-in staging area from where announcements are made; the national anthem is played; and dignitaries, BAA officials, and former champions are recognized and fire the gun to start the various races and waves. Additional barricades, ropes, and other equipment line the course to increase safety, such as in Ashland where a traffic island briefly separates runners to each side.

In 1981, when local U.S. Olympic favorite and two-time winner Johnny "The Elder" Kelley was going to start Boston for the 50th time since 1928— having not finished only 3 times up to that point—it was decided to recognize this record feat with a sign in Hopkinton. Paul "Buzzy" Buswell contacted his friend Jacques "Jack" LeDuc, who not only created a sign but also was tapped for more. The creative LeDuc thought about the uninspired start line, which lacked any distinct artistry. With permission from the Hopkinton Marathon Committee, he added to a thicker white line the BAA logo and borders of green, among other touches. Despite the fact someone later covertly covered it in white paint, which forced a reapplication by LeDuc, thus began a welcomed and anticipated colorful tradition.

"I created a sign to honor Johnny Kelley on what would be his 50th Boston Marathon. Quite a milestone," recalled LeDuc. "The newly created

The first Jack LeDuc–painted Boston Marathon start line, in 1981. *Courtesy Jack LeDuc.*

Hopkinton Marathon Committee had a total operating budget of $500. Most, if not all, was to pay for a volunteer lunch after the race went off. My friend Buzzy went to a committee meeting to get a permit for our CB (citizens band) club to sell food on the common the day of the race. While he sat listening, they mentioned wanting to create a sign and he volunteered me, saying 'we' would do it for free. After the Marathon at their follow-up meeting, they invited me [there] to thank me and asked if there was something else I could do to help. I stated that people from all over the world come to see the start of the Marathon, but there was nothing but a simple white, nondescript stripe in the road. I offered to 'dress it up' a bit. And that began a tradition to last decades."

Of all the tangible elements that comprise the historic route, it is the one that is kindly mistreated and trampled for several hours by thousands of people. The multicolored start line stretches 39 feet from curb to curb across East Main Street and spans on average approximately 244 square feet. It is, quite literally, where it all starts. And ideally, sometime within the week leading up to the race is when the festooned paint job begins.

"My first co-conspirator was, of course, Buzzy. We worked together for quite a few years. Then I asked Dr. Charles Bobeck, who was a member of our committee representing the board of health in town. That team lasted a few years," noted LeDuc. "And as the design morphed to become a little more elaborate, I asked my daughters Laura LeDuc McGee and Jeanne LeDuc Bloom to join me as two extra sets of eyes and keep me grounded while [I was] holding up traffic, answering questions from the media, and making sure I didn't do anything I wouldn't be able to undo. Later, Jeanne's husband, Jonathan, came and helped. Even Matt, Laura's husband, came to lend a hand as well. From a very young age, my wife Karen would bring my daughters up and I would stop halfway through the job to let the paint dry and we would enjoy lunch together. There's a picture of the girls shaking the cans of paint. Great memories."

Even LeDuc's mother, Marie Simonne LeDuc; his sisters Carolle Lawson and Francine Harrel; and one of the race director's sons, Ryan McGillivray, helped over the years.

"My mother Simonne would walk from home and bring me snacks and water. She was so proud of me for doing something so relatively simple," said LeDuc.

As with all outdoor events, weather is certainly a factor, especially when painting. And April in New England rarely cooperates.

"We shoot for the Wednesday before [the race] and watch the forecast," LeDuc said. "The first few years we would apply the base coat of white with a nine-inch roller. After a while, the Hopkinton DPW would come up and spray the base with the same equipment they use to paint the crosswalks in town. Later, Accurate Lines out of Needham would put down the base on a schedule to fit the painting of the mile and kilometer markings along the course. But I [went] full circle and painted the base with a roller. And we

Top: Early Boston Marathon finish lines included a single white line on Exeter Street, as in 1935, with a victorious Johnny "The Elder" Kelley. *Courtesy of the Boston Public Library, Leslie Jones Collection.*

Bottom: The 2005 Boston Marathon start line honoring two-time winner Johnny "The Elder" Kelley. *Photo by Paul Clerici.*

have painted as late as the day before [such as] in 1996. Without a question, the most memorable—if you want to call it that—in my involvement has to be the event leading up to the 100th running of the Boston Marathon. The big dance! I'm talking about the [multiple] inches of wet, heavy snow that occurred on the Wednesday before what was supposed to be the biggest celebration of marathon history since the original battle."

The painted area of the centennial start line was the largest in its history up to that point. While the length of the start line never changes from its 13 yards from side to side, the width—or thickness—of the start line has changed. On average, it ranges between 5 and 6 feet. But not for the centennial.

"On the 100th running in 1996, the line was 100 inches thick. That grew until the 106th running, where it measured 106 inches," LeDuc pointed out. "But in 1996, the first time ever the BAA was to open the course to (nearly 40,000) participants, I had agreed to paint the start and the finish lines. Needless to say, time was running out and it took a few days for the snow to melt at the appropriate locations. On the day I had planned to paint the start line, we received eight inches of wet, heavy snow. I had two lines

Creating the Boston Marathon start line in 1996 for its 100th edition are Jack LeDuc (*far left*), Dr. Charles Bobeck (*kneeling*), and Paul Buswell (*far right*). *Courtesy Jack LeDuc.*

Boston Marathon finish-line elements expanded in 1996 to accommodate and celebrate the race's centennial. *Photo by Frank Clerici Sr.*

to paint and was held hostage by Mother Nature. I showed up with my helpers, Doc and Buzzy, at the start on the Saturday before the race, only to receive a call from Boston that Boylston Street was dry and ready to be painted. They had already scheduled the police detail and we had to paint the finish that day. So, with my crew in tow, supplies in the back of the truck, we rushed to my house to trade the start stencils for the finish [stencils] and headed into Boston. We were able to complete the task but in the back of my mind, 'what about the start line?' Luckily, the next day, Sunday, albeit cool, we were able to paint East Main Street in Hopkinton. We had to set up barricades to prevent the bus loads of tourists from stepping on the wet paint. We actually learned the Chinese word for wet that day (from tourists). So by some miracle of miracles, both lines were ready for the next day—the 100th running of the Boston Marathon."

Unique painted additions to the start line each year also could be found in little personal touches that LeDuc incorporated. Along with the requisite START and accompanying date, logos, and names, he painted other images, including depictions of the course, elevation, and various landmarks; nods to a record or anniversary, as in 2012 with a runner's bib number 40 to mark the years women have officially run Boston; or tributes to honor the passing of someone special, such as when Johnny "The Elder" Kelley died in October 2004.

"I sketched, cut, and painted a likeness of his face in the middle of the start line the following April," LeDuc said of Kelley. "When Jock Semple passed away—the longtime trainer and coach of the BAA—I attempted to memorialize him ahead of the line with a black laurel wreath with his initials in the middle. And when Harold 'Lefty' Rathburn, a former board of governor to the BAA who preceded me as the start-line announcer for many years, passed, I like to feel we honored him by painting a graphic of a microphone with his initials under it. In addition, I try to keep the start line topical. In 1991, when we were at war in the Middle East, I applied a large American flag which appeared to fly under the start line. And when we went from a single start to a two-wave start, we displayed a continuous wave across the start line with the colors that represented the waves—red and blue."

There was even a time when LeDuc painted both the start and finish lines, the latter of which for only a handful of years in the 1990s, lastly in 1999.

"It didn't exactly match the start line, but I used the same font. [And] white letters on a yellow base. It turned out to be a bad choice. I hadn't taken into account the position of the sun at two p.m. when the top runners would be finishing and the cameras wouldn't be able to read the word FINISH. Good catch by then-race director Guy Morse," recalled LeDuc. "So, it was back to Boston and magically the white letters now showed brightly in blue. [And] in the early years I used corrugated cardboard from Buzzy's employer. Then I turned to quarter-inch plywood to create the stencils."

After 37 years, from 1981 to 2017, LeDuc retired from his street-painting duties, with the 121st Boston as his last canvas.

"After the nerve-racking experience with the 100th behind me, I decided that was it. I couldn't count on two days in mid-April to be ideal weather-wise, so I stopped painting the finish line [then]," he said. "I was actually one of only a few people I knew that dreaded the coming of spring; coming up with a topical design—something that wouldn't resemble previous years—and laying out and cutting stencils."

RoadSafe Traffic Systems, out of Avon, which took over painting the finish line when LeDuc stopped, did likewise after the artist fully retired his rollers and stencils, in 2018, the fifth anniversary of the 2013 bombings.

Bib F40 alongside the 2012 Boston Marathon start line to mark the 40th anniversary of the first year women were allowed, by the governing body AAU, to run in the race in 1972. *Photo by Paul Clerici.*

"There is definitely an uptick in the number of people visiting the start and finish lines to snap a photo or just to spend a moment reflecting on what happened here [in 2013]," observed RoadSafe marketing manager James Hurley. "My crew and I are so honored to be part of this. They do an amazing job."

This is a common sight in the days leading up to Boston: tourists and runners having their pictures taken near the colorful Hopkinton attraction. It happens so often, especially throughout the weekend of the race, that town police gladly stop vehicular traffic to allow for the opportune snapshot.

On Patriots' Day, as participants make their way along the course to the finish, they trek over several four-square-foot painted yellow mile and kilometer markers near the yellow center traffic lines and countless white BAA unicorn logos and water station markers (for the separate elite and non-elite stations) closer to the sidewalks where the station tables are assembled. Unlike with most other marathons, there is no painted blue line on the course, as it was deemed it would be too confusing for drivers the rest of the year. In charge of all those applications is Accurate Lines Inc. in Needham.

"[We use] yellow and white traffic paint, and it takes two people to paint them. We have been painting the Boston Marathon since 1980," noted Accurate Lines co-owner and president Bill Sayman. "It is rewarding and has become a tradition."

Boston Marathon race director and DMSE (Dave McGillivray Sports Enterprises) founder and president Dave McGillivray oversees and monitors these public roads through eight communities. It is no small task, of course, as the entire outdoor surface for this event is in constant use year-round.

"I personally conduct or attend roughly about 150 meetings," he said. "We have about 90 people on the organizing committee and we have 8,000 volunteers. I usually delegate to various organizing committee members, but there are timelines and planning phases along the way that we have to adhere to. I always set false advance deadlines to be sure I get things well before I need them. Doesn't always work, but most of the time it does."

The heart of the Boston Marathon planning is an unassuming-looking yet all-encompassing three-ring bible that details every aspect involved: schedules, lists, names, timelines, contacts, phone numbers, backups, contingency plans. Everything!

"It is called the Operation Manual," McGillivray noted. "Now, everyone contributes their 'work' (documents) and we simply put them all in one manual. Very helpful to use as a reference and to ensure that all the work has been completed."

Boston Marathon technical producer Edward Jacobs, president of Interstate Rental Service Inc., maintains an extremely detailed nine-page checklist ledger called Gameplan Boston. Not only does it list nearly every requirement involved to build the Boston Marathon, but it also includes a daily layout of jobs and tasks to be executed by whom and by when. The first entry in his 12-day hourly schedule of must-haves that lead to the race is usually "posting No Parking signs," and the final item is "the removal of all materials."

Race day itself occupies nearly four pages. Nothing—no matter how seemingly insignificant—is left for chance. One routine job repeated throughout the timeline is listed as "tag and tow"—the laborious tagging and towing of vehicles. This is a major undertaking in the city of Boston on any day of the week, but especially so with the world coming to town and extra room being needed for workers to remove street signs, light posts, newspaper vending machines, park benches, and even a bus stop. While this is occurring, workers also construct bleachers, crowd-control barricades, grandstands, and cement Jersey barriers.

Regarding aid stations on the course, elite runners are provided with eight, which feature mostly their own pre-filled bottles of fluid that are often marked with colorful designs, country flags, or other discernable attachments

The 1980 version of the Boston Marathon finish line with two colors—yellow and red—and Boston AA Marathon (Boston Athletic Association Marathon) and Prudential Center (the finish location at the Prudential Center Building) on Ring Road. *Photo by Paul Clerici.*

in order to be easily seen from a distance. There are also 25 water and sports drink stations available for all runners.

"They're on two sides of the road, nine tables on each side, three cups per person in the race, and about 80–100 volunteers per station," detailed McGillivray of the layout, whose staggered placement at each mile is designed to eliminate the inevitable bottleneck if stations were situated directly across each other. In addition, the course is sporadically lined with medical tents, portable toilets, and cooling stations (when required).

In recent years, the overall on-course image of the race has been in sync with signage by AMI Graphics of New Hampshire. The cohesive look includes everything from corral signs for each wave; standing mile and kilometer markers that accompany timing clocks; vertical markers at each station; and directional banners at turns and the finish.

"Years ago, the event signage was limited to the finish line and some direction signs. Today, the program has grown to several thousand individual signs being used on race weekend," said Mike Chamberas, former BAA consultant/liaison. "I feel very fortunate to [have been] part of such an historic event and important organization. I also enjoy looking back at how the signage program has grown."

While connecting nearly 60 miles of barricades to fence in the entire course on both sides would prove prohibitive, Jacobs nevertheless utilizes a combined total of more than 5,000 8-foot and 10-foot crowd barricades throughout the course—1,200 at the start; 1,000 on the course; 3,000 at the finish. Additionally, there are certain measures taken by each town and city on the course to line and secure their portion of the route.

Starting the first of April each year, the Ashland DPW begins to transform its share of Route 135, which includes the rare traffic islands in the middle of the early miles.

"[We] fill potholes; install orange and white stanchions around islands; tape off islands with police caution tape; make sure structures such as manholes and water gates are not trip hazards; set up roadblocks using wood barricades at a dozen locations; [and] line-paint the course, if necessary," lists Ashland DPW director Doug Small, who added that it takes about 30 barricades and 200 cones and stanchions to do the job. "[We also] set up cooling stations at various locations, if necessary, due to the heat; and pick up litter before and after the race."

In Natick, while barriers are also placed at every intersection over its four-plus miles of the course, work commences months before race day in order to be Marathon ready.

"About 40 barricades and signs [are used, and] we place the message boards in advance of the event," said former Natick Director of Public

Traffic island in the Ashland portion of the Boston Marathon. *Photo by Paul Clerici.*

Works Bill Chenard. "The work begins as soon as the snow is gone. We sweep and clean the course, paint the lines. Just prior to the Marathon, we clean the entire route. Total staff is typically about 12."

Some of the most popular and recognizable portions of the Marathon—the *Young at Heart* statue of Johnny "The Elder" Kelley, Heartbreak Hill, Boston College—are located in Newton, which comprises 13 villages. (The course runs through four: Newton, Newton Lower Falls, West Newton, and Chestnut Hill). And as temporary host to thousands of college students who make their home in the Newtons, a unique aspect of race prep is the constant maintenance of the roadways and greeneries that are well-traveled for months before the Marathon.

"We repave or fix damaged pavement and curbs; the grassy areas along the road will be reseeded; and loam borders will be checked and fixed," said former acting Newton transportation director Nina Wang.

Closer to the race, as well as on Patriots' Day, Newton's police, fire, recreation, and public works departments join several other crews—sweeper, trash, traffic, and so on—to cover the four villages.

"The line painting will be refreshed before the race—these include the center lines, lane lines, and crosswalks. Sweeper crews will sweep the street on the day before. Trash crews will install trash bags and barrels along the route," said Wang. "Traffic crews start working at four a.m. and will post 300 No Parking/Tow Zone signs along the route and side streets leading to the route for fire access, and deliver [and set up] about 200 wooden barricades the day before at key intersections for road closures during the race. There are caution tapes/ropes spread along the curb of the roadways for crowd control, and they set up 430-plus European (metal) barricades along the route."

Even though the Marathon runs through Brookline for only just over a mile of Beacon Street, that span of roadway is a highly congested portion of the course. It includes the MBTA subway cars and tracks of the Cleveland Circle Green Line; densely populated neighborhoods; and with only about a 5K remaining, an ideal dropout location.

"We set up barricades at all intersection streets along the race route, and we also provide a rope barrier along the sidewalk to keep pedestrians off the route," said Brookline Highway, Sanitation, and Fleet Maintenance director Kevin Johnson. "The management team starts meeting two months prior. Twenty-five DPW employees [are] directly involved with the preparation and setup on Marathon day [with] 180 barricades, 200 metal barricades, 12,000 feet of nylon rope, 150 No Parking signs, two rubbish trucks, and three street sweepers."

While fire apparatuses, ambulances, and police vehicles can obviously cut through the course in response to emergency situations, many nonemergency residential services such as water and sewer are still a concern that must be addressed by all the towns.

"It is important to have water and sewer personnel stationed on the north and south sides of Route 135 [in Ashland] during the race," noted Small.

This is also a concern for Johnson around miles 23–24 in Brookline.

"We need to stage two water and sewer personnel and equipment on the north side of Beacon Street to be able to respond to any emergency that may occur during the Marathon," Johnson said. "We do this because there is no way to cross Beacon Street while the Marathon is ongoing. There are several meetings with police, fire, and DPW to ensure public safety on this day."

Similar preparations can also be found in Hopkinton, Framingham, Wellesley (including Wellesley Lower Falls), and Boston (including Brighton, Kenmore Square, Back Bay, and Copley Square).

The entire course is also traversed periodically leading up to the Marathon to ensure the roads are safe. And scheduled the morning before the race, at one o'clock, is the street-cleaning crew. Street sweepers are driven from

For the 490 Battle of Marathon in Greece, a 2500th anniversary logo (*top right*) and wreath olive branch (*left*) adorn the 2010 Boston Marathon start line. *Photo by Paul Clerici.*

Hopkinton to Boston, as well as on the 3.1-mile route of the BAA 5K that takes place Sunday morning. This is also one of the last chances to report and repair any road-surface problems, a regular procedure that begins weeks earlier.

"A few weeks out, I run most of the course myself on my last training run," said McGillivray, a Boston Marathon Quarter Century Club "streaker" since 1973. "I also try to drive in a few weeks out to check it. And, of course, many others on the staff and committee inspect it."

Even after all the stipulated checks and rechecks, there are still close calls. One in particular occurred when a water main pipe burst in the Coolidge Corner area of Beacon Street in Brookline near the 24-mile mark. Immediately contacted were several agency reps, including Amy Dominici (former state and federal liaison to the BAA, under Boston's secretary of public safety); former assistant adjutant general David Gavigan of the Massachusetts Army National Guard; the Massachusetts Highway Department; and the MBTA, because the century-old pipe broke early on Patriots' Day Monday, April 17, 1995—the very morning of the race.

"I received the initial call from Brookline Water Department that there was a break in the [water] main underground on the Marathon route," recalled Jacobs. "I responded to the site at approximately four a.m. The street pavement was broken and had risen five feet. I determined we could re-route the course with the breaks in the block before and after the site if we could not get through. Under these circumstances, we would measure the alternate course and report it as appropriate. I called Dave McGillivray and Amy Dominici and notified all state agencies. Amy received calls offering support from state highway, MBTA, etc. [And] Gavigan of the National Guard assigned troops to the site."

The emergency forced the town to cut off the water, which affected area neighbors and businesses with reduced or no water pressure. And a quick decision was required in regard to the passability of the course itself.

"After a conversation with Dave, I let Brookline know we need 15 feet of street width for the lead 'pack' [of runners] to pass through," Jacobs described. "The National Guard called me every 30 minutes to report progress on the width available. By 11:00 a.m., we had the 15 feet we needed. The troops stayed there and surrounded the damaged roadway to guide the runners through. All went well."

Fortunately for everyone involved, the 1995 Boston was still under the noontime start and 11:45 a.m. wheelchair start instead of the current schedule of multiple early-morning starts.

"We were able to reduce the impacted area enough to allow the necessary 15 feet of roadway at that point in the race to allow runners to pass," McGillivray said, and then cautiously added, "Now, if that happened at Mile 3! Hmmm, that would have been a very different challenge!"

The most congested space is a three-block stretch of Boylston Street, between intersecting Exeter and Berkeley Streets. That clustered area includes the finish line, 2,000-seat bleachers, 280-seat grandstands (with wheelchair access ramps), media tents, postrace supplies, emergency services, family meeting areas, and baggage buses. There are also several large tents with concrete anchors for VIPs and medical personnel, the latter of which are designed as emergency triage units with two main tents of 60x220 feet (with 200 cots) and 30x170 feet (with 80 cots).

"Each [medical tent] has electric, lighting, hot and cold running water, heat, and air conditioning as needed," Jacobs said. "At the 2012 Boston Marathon, with temps approaching 90, we brought in more than 200 tons capacity HVAC (Heating, Ventilation, Air Conditioning) of air conditioning and accompanying generators. We were able to hold the main medical tent at 74 degrees. The attached 20x80-foot cooling area was maintained at 62 degrees."

Peeled-off laminated Boston Marathon finish line on a display wall at the expo in 2006. *Photo by Paul Clerici.*

These finish-line setups also aided those affected by the 2013 bombings. According to former Boston Public Health Commission communications director Nick Martin, while three spectators succumbed to fatal injuries and were not transported to hospitals, 265 people who suffered nonfatal (but critical, serious, fair, or other) injuries were either administered to at those tents or were transported to 27 local and area hospitals.

Slightly out of view are mobile command centers, forklifts, trailers, and golf carts. And usually hidden in and behind various structures are a myriad of electrical wiring, phone lines, cables, transformers, and generators. Also, closer to race day is the rerouting of select public transportation services of bus lines and the subway.

"There are roughly 12 operations trailers and mobile units placed at the command compound. They all get electric—shore and backup generators, hardwire telephone, and Internet," said Jacobs. "They share a common internal paging talkback system. This accommodates BAA operations, Boston Police, Boston Fire, Boston EMS, Boston Transportation, MEMA (Massachusetts Emergency Management Agency), State Police, National Guard, and CST (military Civil Support Team)."

High above the finish line is the media bridge from where the race is primarily televised and photographed. The colorful structure is a beacon to the runners who can see the celebrated finish marker the moment they exit Hereford Street onto Boylston Street about four blocks away.

"The photo bridge is built to accommodate vehicular traffic. Clearance underneath is 16 feet. Total [occupancy] of approximate 100 media, including live TV with talent, video, and still photographers," described Jacobs. "Takes two nights to build. We close the road Friday and Saturday from midnight to 6:00 a.m. Comes down before midnight on race day. Same with the announcers and officials position."

The coup de grace, so to speak, is the majestic and commanding finish line itself. But in actuality, there are two of them. Unlike in the early years when it was painted for race day, the finish line now is a rolled-out version applied days before. At 329 square feet, the multicolored strip is 7 feet thick by 47 feet from sidewalk to sidewalk. Since 1970, this job has been assigned to Interstate Rental Service, whose workers annually clean off that portion of Boylston Street in front of the Boston Public Library (BPL) and unroll and adhere the shiny new photo op.

"The finish line is a laminated, adhesive-back, digitally-printed 3M product. It is produced in panels," Jacobs explained. "We lay it down on Saturday, unless weather dictates different."

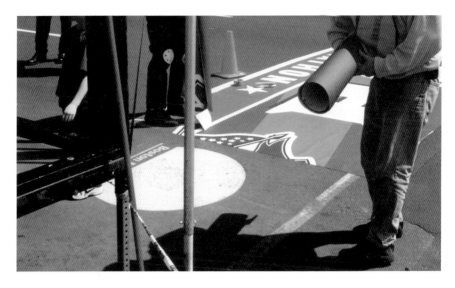

Boston Marathon laminated application of the finish line on Boylston Street. *Photo by Paul Clerici.*

Interestingly, that laminated covering is the finish line for only a few days. The finish line seen the rest of the year is the permanent smaller painted version hidden underneath. "It's not painted until the day after the race," McGillivray laughed, "believe it or not."

In the early-morning darkness of Boston two days after the race and the removal of the laminated covering, RoadSafe Traffic Systems of Avon paints the finish. Weather permitting, of course, just before three o'clock, highway safety traffic designers begin their clandestine proceedings.

"We try to get here before the street cleaners because they use water, and we'd have to wait for it to dry," noted highway safety traffic designer Will Belezos one year, as he stood on Boylston Street and watched the city street sweeper divert itself away at three o'clock. "We beat them [this time]. We win!" he added with a laugh.

Police shut down Boylston Street between Dartmouth and Exeter Streets. Workers spread out stencils on the road and then carefully measure and draw chalk markings at various spots along the edge of the finish line so the letters and numbers can be re-created in the exact locations.

"We chalk the letters on the street because when we cover [the finish line] in the yellow paint, it will cover everything," said highway safety traffic designer Eric House of that one very brief period of time when the finish line is entirely yellow with no words.

The next step includes the revelation of the secret names of each paint color that is ultimately seen by millions of people throughout the year. Three separate Titan Speeflo Powrliner 6900XLT line striper machines are filled with Franklin Paint Co. Hydrophast Waterborne Traffic Paint called…2015 Yellow, 2023 Black, 2014 White, 2024 Blue. Yes, the Boston Marathon finish line is made up of ordinary traffic paint identified by numbers.

"Yeah, that's it," chuckled House. "The same traffic paint that's used everywhere. But it dries fast. Takes about 20 minutes, half-hour [per coat], so we get the next color ready."

Approximately six gallons of yellow paint are applied to the 343-square-foot finish line, which measures 7x49 feet. While that dries, five 3-foot letter stencils that comprise the word FINISH (using the letter I stencil twice) are lined up according to the chalk markings. Once the paint dries, workers stand at each end of the finish line and snap a string chalk line that leaves a temporary 49-foot-long level mark on which each letter is lined up and painted blue. That procedure is repeated for three more stencils for the anniversary year, BOSTON, and MARATHON.

The BAA unicorn logo and race name at each end of the finish line require three separate overlapping stencils, as each element is a different color. After

Boston Marathon finish line being freshly painted in the early-morning hours a few days after the race. *Photo by Paul Clerici.*

Above: A closed Boylston Street a few days after the Boston Marathon so the finish line can be painted. *Photo by Paul Clerici.*

Opposite: Boston Marathon finish line with the logo of presenting sponsor Bank of America, in 2023. *Photo by Paul Clerici.*

each three-foot letter for FINISH dries, the shadowing elements that give it that 3D appearance are painstakingly cut out of cardboard flats and then painted white. Finally, two thin lines of black paint are laid down to frame the finish line. Touchups to correct color bleedings or mistakes are handled by hand with a brush or towel. The job takes an estimated eight gallons of paint, a dozen stencils, three line stripers, two workers, and about three hours.

LeDuc "fondly" recalled (before RoadSafe) the first time he painted the start and finish lines. Unfamiliar with the streets of Boston then, and with all the stencils and paint in his truck, he only knew that the finish line was somewhere near the BPL. As LeDuc drove closer to where he thought it was located, he noticed a police officer and asked for directions.

"I asked him where's the Boston Public Library, and he says, 'It's right near the Boston Marathon finish line.' And I said, 'No, it isn't. I have the finish line in the back of my truck!'" he noted with a laugh. "And when I finally got there and was on my hands and knees painting it, I see a pair of dress shoes come up to me, and he says, 'Don't you need a detail?' And I said, 'No, I have it.'"

LeDuc then looked up and noticed it was another officer, who was kindly "offering" him a police detail since he was already blocking traffic.

Weather also pushed it to the limit once when Accurate Lines was forced to paint the finish line on Patriots' Day itself.

"One year, we painted (laminated) the finish of the Marathon the day of the race and the first wave [had] already started when we were painting," recalled Sayman. "It was due to the rain the whole week before, and [we] couldn't get clearance until the day of."

The Boston Marathon finish line on Boylston Street has grown large enough to be clearly seen from high above. *Photo by Paul Clerici.*

Tying it all together, from start to finish, is the ubiquitous signage located throughout the course. From the Boston Marathon Athletes' Village to the start, from the course to the finish, there must be conveyed a single overall design.

"One very important aspect of the job is creating and maintaining a consistent message to the participants and spectators," noted Chamberas, whose consultant/liaison position had been to ensure the BAA's vision of a consistent look—color, font, logo, and so on—was executed at all venues. "The scope of my services [was] not limited to just the race course, but also the signage related to events surrounding the race; for example, from sponsor signage at the expo to specific signage for the elite athlete hydration stations. In the role, I interface[d] with internal BAA staff, outside consultants, sponsors, and the signage vendor."

But even the best laid plans do not always promise great success for an outdoor event. The Boston Marathon has experienced everything from sleet (1907), a partial eclipse (1939), snow (1961, 1967), and record heat (1905, 1909, 1976) to torrential rain (1970). Closer to McGillivray's tenure were snow-drenched fields of the Athletes' Village for its centennial (1996), low-ceiling dense mist (2002), a near-race-cancellation rainstorm (2007), extreme heat that prompted the BAA for the first time to offer deferrals (2012), and steady, cold wind-driven rain and wind (2018).

"[That] hit most of them!" he noted of the list. "We've been lucky. In my [many] years, not too many challenging issues; but again, most of them have to do with the weather, and there is not a lot we can do about that other than to 'gear up' for what is being forecasted. [In 1996] we brought in hay bales, woodchips, and had NG (Northrop Grumman military) helicopters hover low to help dry off the fields! [The 2007 rainstorm] was brutal, mainly the tough decision to go or no go, and it was based on the final forecast, that likely things were going to 'die down' a bit—and they did. And if they didn't? Well, I'd probably be saying now, 'So, do you want fries with that burger?' [For the record heat, we] just continued to ramp up the medical coverage all along the course."

With such adverse experiences under his belt, McGillivray maintains a few essentials: for the "weather to cooperate, even though we have no control over that one; everyone carry out their jobs as planned; and I wake up on the morning on time and don't oversleep!"

And amazingly, by the next morning's commute, most traces of the Boston Marathon—save for painted remnants and an occasional barrier—are all put away for next year.

3

FINISHER MEDALS

Historically speaking, the presentation of a medal can be traced to the second century BC, when Seleucid Empire ruler Alexander I Theopator Euergetes Balas awarded Jonathan the High Priest with a "golden button," according to *The Genuine Works of Flavius Josephus the Jewish Historian* writings of the AD 37–100 historian. Since then, medals have been routinely awarded for extraordinary merit in a variety of fields.

The Boston Athletic Association (BAA) has bestowed on its Boston Marathon winners richly decorated diamond-centered medals as one of the champion prizes. In 1983, for the first time in its history, finisher medals were handed out as well.

The idea of finisher medals arose in late 1982, during the time when the Boston Marathon's future was being determined by the courts in regard to when the race had been "signed over" to an individual (but eventually by the courts returned to the BAA). It was discussed primarily between BAA Board of Governors Tom Brown (president), Tim Kilduff, and Harold Rathburn.

"One of the reasons for the finisher medal is that's when medals were being given at other races and none at Boston. The more we became aware of this stuff, we had to do this," recalled Kilduff, who was also the Boston Marathon race director then (1983–84). "Tom Brown, Harold Rathburn, and I were on the board of governors, and I said that we have to do something about this. And it was Harold that deserves the credit because he called [Ashworth Awards CEO] Doug Ashworth and got it done."

Ashworth Awards of North Attleborough, about 35 miles south of Boston, is within the collective Attleboro town villages once home to up to seven major jewelers, dating back to the 1800s, prompting a billboard that stated "Attleboro: The Hub of the Jewelry World" to be erected in the town.

"Harold Rathburn…had a mutual friend with my father, Douglas Ashworth, who passed away in 2005. Harold was looking for a company that was good with pewter to make medals for the BAA. They met at a restaurant called the Brook Manor in North Attleborough, owned by the Scarlatelli family, and the rest is history," noted Ashworth Awards CEO and president Dan Ashworth. "The Attleboros used to be known as the 'Jewelry Capital of the USA' because we had so many manufactures in the area."

For official finishers, it is a literal badge of honor, especially after spending months, and even years, devoted to that singular goal of the Boston Marathon. For Diane Culhane of Massachusetts, for example, who has run Boston eight times, the medal possesses great significance.

"The medal symbolizes all the hard work that went into preparing for the race," she said. "The endless training runs in hot or cold weather—at all times of the day; the cross-training that went along with the running training, weight training, biking, etc. The medal reflects the accomplishment of our bodies being able to finish such a long race."

Of her eight, one held an even more special familial meaning for Culhane.

"If I remember correctly, my brother Dan [Damish], my father [Ed Damish], and I all ran the same Marathon," she noted of one year. "The excitement was when you got to Hopkinton, there were runners and spectators everywhere! Everywhere you looked, there were reporters interviewing runners. You could taste the excitement in the air. I never saw

BAA Gloria G. Ratti Collection display of Boston Marathon champion and finisher medals, including 1899 winner Lawrence Brignolia's eighth-place medal from the first race in 1897 (*top left*). *Photo by Paul Clerici.*

Above: First finisher medal presented at the Boston Marathon, created by Ashworth Awards, in 1983. *Courtesy Ashworth Awards*.

Opposite: Boston Marathon finisher medals for the 2020 virtual edition. *Courtesy Ashworth Awards*.

my father or brother during the race, but there was a level of comfort during the hard parts knowing that they were also there."

The tangible honor holds unique memories for finishers regardless of if they ran Boston only once or are a Quarter Century Club member (25 consecutive years) because each year is different for its own place in one's life.

"The more times that I successfully compete in Boston, the more my pride grows," said multi-Boston Qualifier Brian Baker of New York. "I've been running Boston since I was first officially allowed at age 19 (in 1981) when I ran 3:23:03. [In] 2023, at age 61, I ran 3:16:36. While my Boston PR is 2:47:02, run in 1984, I feel that from an age-graded standpoint this may

have been my strongest effort to date. I feel very fortunate to be this healthy and still be competing in Boston after [decades] of running. In my opinion, qualifying for Boston is the equivalent of qualifying for the Olympics for us mere mortals. I feel very fortunate that I am still able to do so and that I've run Boston throughout every decade of my life—from my teens to my 60s—and I hope to continue to do so for the rest of my life."

The creative process involved with the first finisher medal was not complex or too time-consuming.

"Doug designed the medal. We gave him the unicorn head, the old [BAA] letterhead, and that's what Ashworth came back with. We didn't get any big proofs or anything; and if they did [have any], it was done between Doug and Harold. Life was simpler then. Now, you'd have to have a committee," Kilduff said with a laugh. "Harold and Doug came back with the first idea, with no color on it, and there was no ribbon. That was it."

Even with the passage of decades since its first issuance, the obverse of the finisher medal has largely remained the same in terms of its unicorn-centered design.

"The unicorn was always the focal point of the medal from the beginning," Ashworth said of the BAA's mythical logo. "This is the story that I have been told, because I was only 14 years old when the first order was placed. Back in the early days, the organizing committee met in a cigar shop. In this shop was a [table] unicorn [lighter] that had a flame that came out of its horn for the customers to light their cigars on. We refurbished this back in the '80s because it was in bad shape. We made a new horn for it, fixed some broken parts, and replated it gold. And now it is a focal point in the BAA office. Each year, the BAA has the same three colors as their primary colors—these are blue, yellow, and white. We try and come up with a new color combination each year or a new feature, such as translucent color fill, etc."

From 1983 to 1995, the pewter-color finisher medal was round and most years attached to a blue/orange-tinged ribbon. The centennial version in 1996 introduced the first polished multicolored solid horseshoe shape, followed in 2016 with a polished cut-out unicorn with open space to each side.

"The medal design does not change often," said Ashworth. "It started as round, then transitioned to the current shape in 1996 for the 100th anniversary. In 2013, to keep up with the trend of larger finisher medals, we increased the size. It has been this size since 2013, except for the 125th anniversary [in 2021, when] it was the largest medal to date."

Despite changes in the finisher medal's shape, size, and color, its familiarity has been a constant.

"My favorite things about the Boston Marathon finisher medal all have to do with its consistency," noted Baker. "After all these years, it still has the leftward facing unicorn, the year, which race it is (such as 2023 being

Boston Marathon finisher medals, dating back to the first year in 1983. *Courtesy Ashworth Awards.*

the 127th), and having Boston Athletic Association all on it. While there are always minor design changes, I feel that consistency over the long run is something that defines a classic and how a classic lives up to its name."

The process by which the finisher medal is created is a precise one to leave nothing to chance.

"Once the design is finalized, these are the steps involved," explained Ashworth. "Create the tooling; cast the medal out of 800-plus-degree melted metal; clean casting and deburr (remove sharp edges); finish casting in the proper finish; color fill the medallions according to the final art; inspect all medals. While the medals are being manufactured, the ribbons are being manufactured in a different facility. Once all of the medals are done and

Boston Marathon finisher medals in the process of being made at Ashworth Awards in North Attleborough, Massachusetts. *Courtesy Ashworth Awards.*

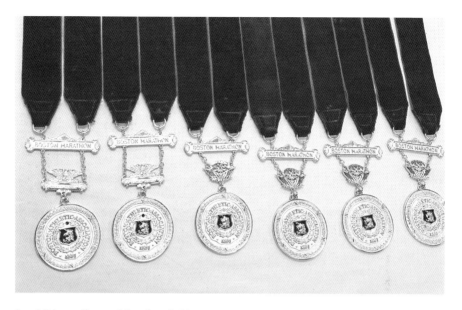

In addition to Boston Marathon finisher medals, Ashworth Awards also makes medals for course records (*first two from left*) and each overall champion for the open and wheelchair categories. *Courtesy Ashworth Awards.*

the ribbons printed, we sew the ribbons directly to the medals. The entire manufacturing process takes about 10 weeks."

For most official finishers, each medal can trigger memories associated with that specific year.

"My very first Boston Marathon, I was casually dating two guys, one who went on to become my husband," recalled Culhane. "However, for that Marathon, they both wanted to be at the finish line! Not knowing what to do, I turned to my girlfriends for advice and got many comical answers—'Just keep running,' 'Turn around and run back!' Luckily, a couple of days before the race, the other guy found out he had to work," she noted with a chuckle. "I ran one of the Marathons on behalf of the Cystic Fibrosis Foundation in honor of one of my husband's relatives who passed at the age of 10 from CF. All of us who were running on the CF team wore pictures on our shirts of those who had CF. Very humbling to be running for someone who could hardly breathe. [And] a huge shutout to the spectators. Their energy keeps you going when all you want to do is stop. I remember going up the hills one year and hearing a spectator cheering his heart out. I had to look up to see who it was and was completely surprised to see that it was someone I knew!"

In addition to the finisher medal, Ashworth Awards also makes other medals for the BAA and has over the years created 40 different versions of the unicorn medallions.

"We manufacture all the medals for all of their events, including the winners' medals for the Marathon. These are manufactured the same way as Olympic medals are. They are sterling silver with gold plate [and] one-tenth carat diamond. The course-record medals are manufactured the same, with a different center and a one-tenth sapphire," said Ashworth. "We manufacture over 40,000 medals for the weekend festivities, including the [BAA] 5K and Marathon. We also manufacture their other specialty items that have included over the years lapel pins, key chains, name badges, lanyards, signage (because we can make large acrylic signs as well), apparel, and whatever other product they may need."

And as proud as are the recipients of the medals, so too are the creators.

"For me personally, and my family, working with the Boston Marathon brings us a tremendous sense of pride," said Ashworth. "It is nice to be able to carry on the tradition my father started with Harold Rathburn back in 1983."

4

RELATIONSHIP WITH OHME-HOCHI 30K
IN JAPAN

Despite the fact that 6,700 miles separate Boston and Ome, the two cities are close due to a decades-long relationship sparked by the sport of running.

In March 1967, in the western Tokyo city of Ome in Japan, was first held the Ohme-Hochi 30K Marathon (spelled as Ohme for the race and only 18.64 miles, not the full marathon's 26.2). In a country where running is truly revered and honored—with its early Olympic Marathon Trials in 1911 and national marathon championships dating back to 1913—traditions are respected with great regard.

With the storied history of the Boston Marathon, which dates to 1897, including six Japanese postwar champions between 1951 and 1969, an international relationship of kindred spirits seemed fatefully inevitable. And so it was on October 15, 1975—with thanks in part to then-Boston race director Will Cloney and sponsoring Tokyo newspaper managing director Yoichi Furukawa—that a mutual agreement was set in place that resulted in the inviting and sending of top athletes to each other's event.

"The relationship continued the Boston tradition of welcoming Japanese athletes to Boston following World War II. The Boston Marathon was the first race to welcome Japanese athletes to the U.S. roads after the war," stated former Boston Athletic Association (BAA) president and executive director Tom Grilk. "They were also kind enough to give an appreciation of Japanese culture to those who visited to compete. For the organizers in Ome, the exchange offered a means to bring some of the Boston tradition to Japan."

In the 1950s, the large Japanese contingent at Boston included four of the top 9 finishers in 1951 (with winner Shigeki Tanaka), four of the top 8 finishers in 1953 (with winner Keizo Yamada in a course-record 2:18:51), three of the top 10 finishers in 1954, three of the top 8 finishers in 1955 (with winner Hideo Hamamura in a CR 2:18:22), two of the top 8 finishers in 1957, and seventh place in 1959.

"They've emulated everything that we've done. It's tremendous!" noted the late BAA vice president Gloria Ratti. "When they came here, they observed and brought back all these ideas—ceremonies, pasta party, race program, results book. And they devote a lot of newspaper coverage to it."

The Ohme Athletic Association (OAA), established in 1936, and *The Hochi Shimbun* newspaper, which by 15 years predates the 1887-estabished BAA, have co-organized the event since its inception. It was ignited by the success of the 1964 Tokyo Olympic Games, when Japan won 29 medals (16 gold), including Marathon bronze by Kokichi Tsuburaya.

"We Japanese are very proud of [Tsuburaya]," said former *The Hochi Shimbun* promotion director and current Ohme Marathon Foundation

Boston mayor John Hynes congratulates 1953 Boston Marathon winner Keizo Yamada of Japan. *Courtesy of the Boston Public Library, Leslie Jones Collection.*

director Masaru Otake, via interpreting by former Japan Association of Athletics Federations (JAAF) official Yoshibumi Honda.

After the 1964 Tokyo Games, the JAAF "decided to strengthen and brush up [the] level of long-distance runners," said Otake, through Honda. "[OAA] proposed [Ome] to JAAF as site of road-runners training site. Because Ome city has such good surrounding and training site, [and] also *The Hochi Shimbun* has similar idea to promote athletes' development program, [this was the] best timing to promote marathon together with Olympic athletes such as Kokichi Tsuburaya with fun-runners. At that time, there is no definition of 'road race' in Japan, so [we] used 'marathon' on behalf of full marathon [to partially name the Ohme-Hochi 30K]."

With that increase of national support, Japanese runners in the 1960s continued to excel at Boston, which included an impressive five of the top six finishers in 1965 (with a podium sweep, including winner Morio Shigematsu in a CR 2:16:33), the top four in 1966, three of the top eight finishers in 1967, and the winner in 1969 (Yoshiaki Unetani in a CR 2:13:49).

In the 1970s, the U.S. governing-body Amateur Athletic Union (AAU) officially allowed women to run in sanctioned races, which included Boston. China-born Michiko "Miki" Suwa Gorman, who grew up in Japan's Fukushima Prefecture with her Japanese parents before they moved to America in 1964, twice won Boston, in 1974 (CR 2:47:11) and 1977 (masters CR 2:48:33); and Japanese women were also in the top 10 in 1976 (eighth) and 1978 (sixth).

With such great success, along with six Boston men's titles between 1951 and 1969, it was in the fall of 1975 when Ohme reached out to Boston as a way to show their thanks, appreciation, and respect.

"They understood the significance of running in Boston—[even] early on back in the '70s—and how important the event was to running worldwide," explained Guy Morse III, BAA race/executive/external affairs director, from 1985 to 2012. "They formalized the agreement so that they could plan it every year to make sure that it would happen because people change, personnel changes, company changes. But the agreement was maintained so that there was the framework every year to make sure it happened."

At first, only each race's winner received the invitation to the other race and was accompanied by an athletic association representative. That criteria changed over the years to include broader opportunities for other athletes to compete.

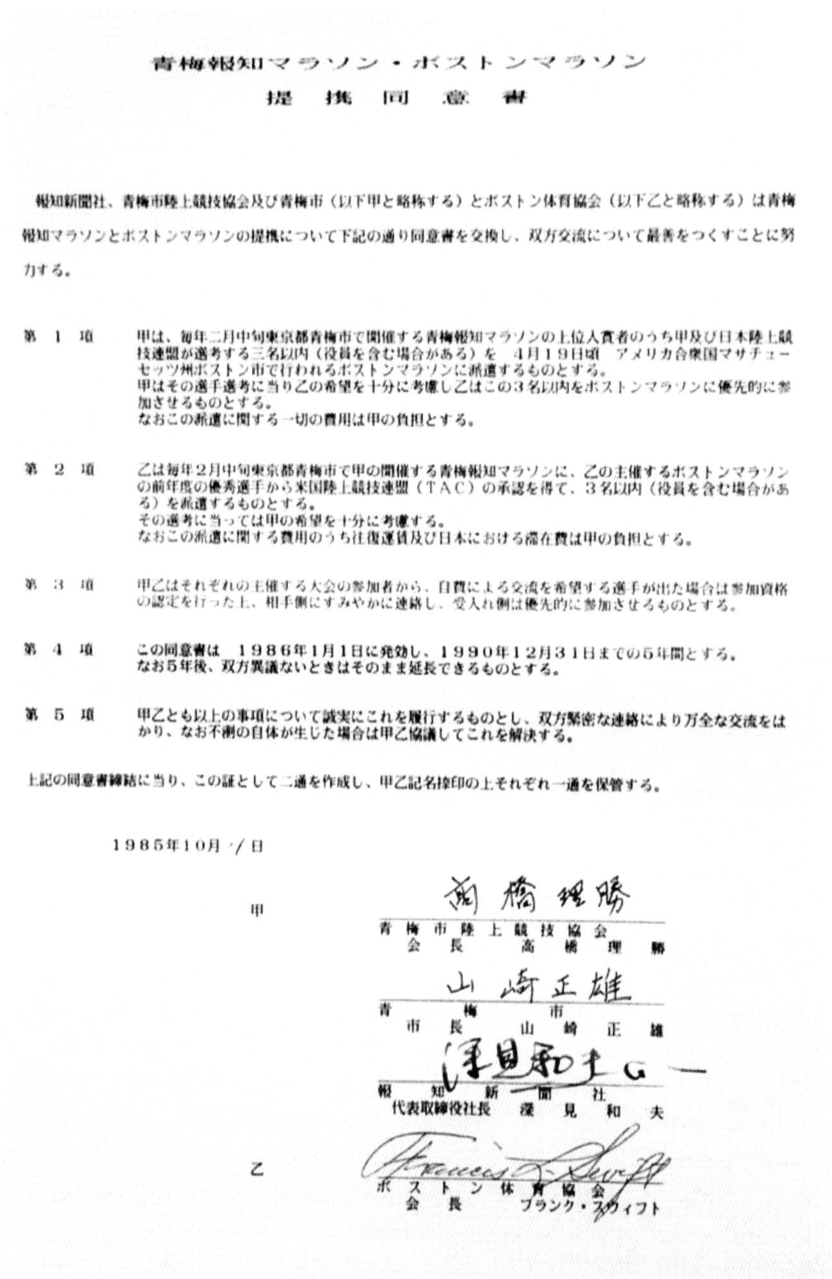

青梅報知マラソン・ボストンマラソン
提 携 同 意 書

報知新聞社、青梅市陸上競技協会及び青梅市（以下甲と略称する）とボストン体育協会（以下乙と略称する）は青梅報知マラソンとボストンマラソンの提携について下記の通り同意書を交換し、双方交流について最善をつくすことに努力する。

第 1 項　甲は、毎年二月中旬東京都青梅市で開催する青梅報知マラソンの上位入賞者のうち甲及び日本陸上競技連盟が選考する三名以内（役員を含む場合がある）を 4月19日頃 アメリカ合衆国マサチューセッツ州ボストン市で行われるボストンマラソンに派遣するものとする。
　　　　甲はその選手選考に当り乙の希望を十分に考慮し乙はこの3名以内をボストンマラソンに優先的に参加させるものとする。
　　　　なおこの派遣に関する一切の費用は甲の負担とする。

第 2 項　乙は毎年2月中旬東京都青梅市で甲の開催する青梅報知マラソンに、乙の主催するボストンマラソンの前年度の優秀選手から米国陸上競技連盟（TAC）の承認を得て、3名以内（役員を含む場合がある）を派遣するものとする。
　　　　その選考に当っては甲の希望を十分に考慮する。
　　　　なおこの派遣に関する費用のうち往復運賃及び日本における滞在費は甲の負担とする。

第 3 項　甲乙はそれぞれの主催する大会の参加者から、自費による交流を希望する選手が出た場合は参加資格の認定を行った上、相手側にすみやかに連絡し、受入れ側は優先的に参加させるものとする。

第 4 項　この同意書は 1986年1月1日に発効し、1990年12月31日までの5年間とする。
　　　　なお5年後、双方異議ないときはそのまま延長できるものとする。

第 5 項　甲乙とも以上の事項について誠実にこれを履行するものとし、双方緊密な連絡により万全な交流をはかり、なお不刺の自体が生じた場合は甲乙協議してこれを解決する。

上記の同意書締結に当り、この証として二通を作成し、甲乙記名捺印の上それぞれ一通を保管する。

1985年10月 / 日

甲

青 梅 市 陸 上 競 技 協 会
会 長 　 　 高 橋 理 勝

青 梅 市
市 長 　 　 山 崎 正 雄

報 知 新 聞 社
代表取締役社長 　 深 見 和 夫

乙

ボ ス ト ン 体 育 協 会
会 長 　 　 フランク・スウィフト

The 1995 Boston Marathon/Ohme-Hochi 30K Athlete Exchange Program extension agreement, in Japanese. *Courtesy the BAA.*

"It's become not necessarily the winners but someone locally who did well because they [Ohme] really want the Boston connection," said Morse. "It's one of those relationships, like the race itself, that really continues to ebb and flow and evolve over time. So the delegation was small some years and larger other years; men [and] females representing—a real mix over the years. There was no standard to it; it was just whatever felt right any given year. And it was important that the organizations be represented and every year reconnect."

To that point, the BAA selected two Hopkinton High School cross-country runners—senior Amanda Hansen and junior Kayla McCann—to compete in the 2019 Ohme-Hochi 30K's accompanying 10K.

"In my opinion, cultural immersion is the most important and impactful influence in my life," Hansen said. "And to have the opportunity to travel to Japan for a week is incredible."

The BAA chose the student-athletes in part due to the criteria of their "academic, athletic, and community services experience." McCann had also been part of her hometown's traditional pre–Boston Marathon dinner for visiting Kenyan runners.

"We are also involved in the community in that we host many foreign exchange students, including Japanese students each year," she noted of her town and school, "and we are involved with the elite Kenyan runners around the time of the Marathon."

The "Letter of Consent of Affiliation" is purposely worded for changes and adjustments.

"The agreement itself is loosely defined so there's lots of flexibility," Morse noted. "It's amazing that it's decades old [with multiple] five-year agreements!"

Based on results of the 1975 Boston, the first of the agreements, champion Bill Rodgers of the Greater Boston Track Club and third-place finisher Tom Fleming of New Jersey were the first selected to run in the Ohme-Hochi 30K.

"We had so much fun," recalled Rodgers, who two months earlier had also finished third at the 1975 Fukuoka Marathon in Japan. "The Japanese officials from Ohme treated us great—first class! We were treated like kings, baseball stars! We weren't paid any money, as you know in those days, but we would get per diems and they'd take us around to great restaurants [and we'd] get wined and dined. It was just amazing the Japanese history, the society, culture, food, the people."

Rodgers won that 10th annual Ohme-Hochi 30K as the first American to do so; Fleming was third.

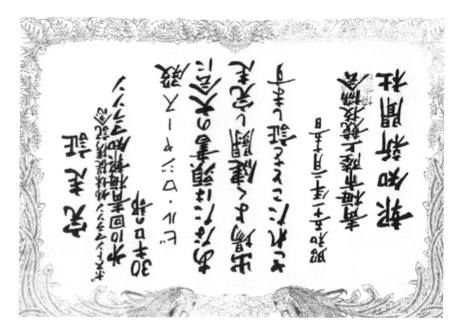

Tenth annual Ohme-Hochi 30K winner Bill Rodgers's 1976 finisher certificate from the Japanese race, sponsored by *The Hochi Shimbun* newspaper and Ohme Athletic Association. Transcribed by Shin Horiuchi, vertical columns from left to right, reads as follows: "*The Hochi Shimbun*. An Association of Track and Field, Ome-City. Showa 51 (1976), Feb. 15th. You participated in the referenced race and successfully finished with great fight, Mr. Bill Rodgers. 30 kilometer race. 10th Ohme-Hochi Marathon. 30 kilometer race. 10 Ohme-Hochi Marathon. An anniversary for the cooperation with the Boston Marathon. Certification of a finisher." *Courtesy Bill Rodgers.*

"I think we were the only Americans—that I know of in the race—and we were contending for the win," recalled Rodgers. "I remember Tom and I coming around the halfway mark and we were in the lead. It's out and back—a pretty tough course—but great weather. It was a great experience."

In the field of nearly 8,000 in the 1976 Ohme-Hochi 30K were 263 women. Of the women who finished, 1974 Boston winner Miki Gorman won. Three months later, the initial Ohme-Hochi 30K contingent who competed in the 1976 "Run for the Hoses" Boston Marathon included Yoshiaki Unetani and Fumikatsu Okita. That inaugural five-year agreement saw Ohme-Hochi 30K wins from Rodgers (1976), Gorman (1976), and Randy Thomas (1980), the latter of whom at the time set a CR 1:30:44. Rodgers, who returned to the Ohme-Hochi 30K in 2006 and ran the accompanying 10K, appreciated Japan's early respect.

"I really got a sense that the Japanese understood the quality of the marathoners is [that of] professional athletes. It wasn't understood in America [then] but it was understood in Japan," Rodgers said. "I really loved that, being a hard-driving marathoner myself. It was a great honor to be representing the U.S. and the BAA when I was there. I took it real serious."

Also within the first five-year pact were several top-10 performances at both races, including Americans Jack Fultz (fifth in 1977), Gary Tuttle (third in 1978), Ronald Wayne (sixth in 1978) at the Ohme-Hochi 30K, and Japan's Yutaka Taketomi (ninth in 1978) at Boston.

As a result of the success of this initial Athlete Exchange Program, it was agreed upon to sign another five-year term and then ad infinitum. Top American visits continued at the Ohme-Hochi 30K with Patti (Catalano) Dillon (1981), Kirk Pfeffer (1982), Greg Meyer (1983), Debbie Mueller (1985), Eileen Claugus (1987), and Jason Lehmkuhle (2011). And top years for Ohme-Hochi 30K athletes at Boston included 1987 for the men (Tomoyuki Taniguchi fifth, Hideki Kita ninth) and 1999 for the women (Mitsuko Sugihara eighth).

Two months after his Ohme-Hochi 30K victory, Meyer also won Boston in 1983.

"It was a great experience," he noted. "I was running really well that winter. I don't know how I got invited, but to me it was my last really hard long tune-up race [for Boston]."

But athletic prowess was—and is—not the sole purpose of the agreement. The social, cultural, and global connections and influences between the two road races, cities, and nations are the real impetuses and rewards.

"Because of our relationship with Ohme," said former BAA president Joann Flaminio, "I have an appreciation of Japanese culture, Japanese art, Japanese customs, Japanese tradition, that I never would have had had I not been exposed to the Ohme marathon road race. I have made lifelong Japanese friends because of our relationship."

Grilk—who lived in Tokyo for a time, was an official representing the BAA at the Ohme-Hochi 30K, and also competed in the race—retains a great affection for Japan.

"Ome, and the neighboring town of Tachikawa, were my children's first introduction to life in Japan, at age 14. They immediately experienced a sense of safety and welcome which continues to mark their view of Japan," he noted.

In 2015, Ome mayor Toshio Takeuchi of Japan (*left*) and BAA president Joann Flaminio sign the Boston Marathon/Ohme-Hochi 30K Athlete Exchange Program five-year extension agreement. *Photo by Paul Clerici.*

Personifying the point of international friendships, Grilk's fondness for Furukawa's generosity still remains long after the Japanese newspaper managing director's passing.

"[He] was one of the most important and endearing elements of my wife's and my years in Japan," Grilk noted. "He personally introduced us to varied and arcane elements of Japanese culture and the arts to which we would never otherwise have had such intimate access—bunraku (puppet theatre); the noh theater and dance; kabuki ('dance-drama'); traditional music with the shamisen (lute) and other ancient instruments; yabusame (running-horse archery); ikebana (flower display); the tea ceremony; origami (paper-folding art); sumo (wrestling); Japanese baseball; and on from these."

Nicholas Arciniaga of Arizona was twice selected to represent the BAA at the Ohme-Hochi 30K, in 2009 and 2015. Each time he visited, he marveled at the culture.

"I didn't know about how they were sister races; that the top guys go out there to run. Once I was selected, I bought a translation book, researched the race course, and I tried to learn as much as I could so I wouldn't slip over any lines of etiquette or anything like that," he said. "The Japanese culture was a big learning experience for me."

Meyer also was unaware of traditional Japanese customs—the exchange of business cards, ceremonial gift-giving, bowing—although he was notified beforehand that he was expected to attend several events as a U.S. and Boston Marathon representative.

"I knew there'd be events that you'd go to, so we brought good clothes and we got there almost a week before," he said. "We actually stayed at a naval base one night and then they took you to this resort at the base of Mount Fuji. It was fabulous! You can't ask for a nicer host than the

At the last pre-pandemic extension agreement ceremony between the Boston Marathon and Ohme-Hochi 30K in Boston, *from left*: BAA vice president Gloria Ratti, Ohme Athletic Association (OAA) director Seikichi Nakamura, Canon Athlete Club Kyushu (CACK) coach Akira Shimizu, Ome mayor Toshio Takeuchi, BAA president Joann Flaminio, CACK athlete Megumi Amako, 2015 Boston Marathon women's open champion Caroline Rotich, 2015 Boston Marathon men's open winner Lelisa Desisa, JR East Running Team (JRERT) athlete Kiyokatsu Hesegawa, JRERT coach Yoshichika Yamada, and OAA vice president Hitoshi Nakano, in 2015. *Photo by Paul Clerici.*

Japanese. But when the [race start] gun goes off, they want to crush you. And that's okay. It was just another race in a different language."

Morse, involved with the BAA in one capacity or another since 1984 and witness to several of the five-year agreements, realized early that this was not just a road-race exchange of athletes.

"The race is very important and it's good for the athletes," he said, "but the relationship between the countries was critically important. The cultural exchange of it became as important as the athletic event itself. It became more than that in terms of the cultural side of the exchange, and likewise when they come [to Boston]."

And that sentiment has remained throughout the decades, as echoed by Flaminio, who has also represented the BAA at Ohme.

"Obviously, the exchange is about a road race. But I think what's been most revealing for me is this notion that the understanding of the different

From left: Ohme Marathon Foundation director and *The Hochi Shimbun* director Masaru Otake, Ohme Athletic Association (OAA) director Kunio Kishino, *The Hochi Shimbun* director Seien Kobayakawa, Ome deputy mayor Horoshi Ikeda, and OAA managing director Yutaka Saito. *Photo by Paul Clerici.*

cultures; [that] we get to go there, they get to come here, and in so doing we not only appreciate the athleticism of the other country, but we also get a better understanding of their culture and their hospitality and their country; how things are different," she points out.

Augmenting that exchange are events that celebrate the relationship. Representatives are expected to speak at some occasions, and itineraries include ceremonial gatherings, media opportunities, gift exchanges, tours, and in the U.S. has included visits to Hopkinton, Cape Cod, museums, a clambake dinner, and even a show in the theater district.

Megumi Amako of Japan, 14th at the 2015 Boston, was selected to run on Patriots' Day via her win two months earlier at the Ohme-Hochi 30K (which had since moved from March to February).

"I was more happy than anything once I found out I was chosen and invited. I knew from before about the relationship before I ran the Ohme marathon," she said through Kay Horiuchi, interpreter for these Japanese runners and whose Japan-born father, Minoru Horiuchi, was a longtime BAA board member and liaison. "This my first time in America. I took it all in. I was taken aback by everything. The city of Boston is beautiful."

Kiyokatsu Hasegawa of Japan, 21st at the 2015 Boston, also thoroughly enjoyed his visit.

"It was beautiful city to run in, especially along the Charles [River]. I was able to run with other people. I was taken to the Legal [Seafood restaurant], and I had lobster, steamers, oysters—I took in the town of Boston!" she said through Kay Horiuchi. "I from such a small area, nobody really knew or thought anything of me coming to Boston. But my parents are so proud of me. I didn't even know how big of a deal I was until I got here. And my parents made special trip and were able to come to this trip. I think they had better time than I did—they went to see Red Sox [baseball game] and had a great trip!"

Regarding gift-giving, some of the items presented by the BAA include Boston Marathon pins and Bay State souvenir gifts that reflect the city's rich history. And gifts from Ohme often include hand-crafted items such as ceramics and plates.

"Very colorful, beautiful, exquisite presentation bowls and smaller bowls all made there," marveled Morse of the Ohme items. "Just beautiful."

In addition to the obvious differences in course length and layout—26.2-mile point-to-point Boston Marathon; 18.64-mile out-and-back Ohme-Hochi 30K—there are many other differences that stand out. For some of the Japanese runners, that includes exuberant spectators or the field size.

Part of the Boston Marathon and Ohme-Hochi 30K exchange program is the presentation of gifts, such as handcrafted ceramic plates from Japan. *Photo by Paul Clerici.*

"In Japan, I think, out of respect, they just being quiet," noted Miharu Shimokado, 12th female at the 2016 Boston. "But in Boston, with all the energy and everything, I ran faster and faster toward the end and I was very excited to hit the finish line."

As for Amako, it was the 2015 Boston field of over 26,000 finishers that caught her attention.

"There was many runners. I was very impressed with how many people were running. I knew it was major feat for me to be coming to Boston and participate in Boston Marathon and I was taken aback with how many people I was going to be running with," she said through Kay Horiuchi.

When Arciniaga first ran the Ohme-Hochi 30K, he knew nothing about the race or the course, so it was all new and different to him.

"I didn't run on the course [beforehand]. We were able to drive over the course the day before," he recalled. "It's basically on a small, two-lane highway going up the side of a mountain and you turn around and come back down. It's a small, one-lane road with 52,000 people into one lane once everybody turns around. It's pretty exciting to race."

Course setups differ as well, from markers, directional signage, support, and even postrace activities.

"The biggest difference for me was the water stations and fueling stations," noted Arciniaga. "They have little Dixie cups that are about two ounces, so I learned to grab two cups at a time because I wasn't expected to get much. And the winner gets a gift from every sponsor of the race! The winner was up there for about 10 minutes getting all the gifts, and he'd have to hand it off to one of his assistants as he was getting them."

The finish-area design was something that also impressed Ratti.

"What amazed me most was the finish line with hundreds of potted chrysanthemum plants lined along the way," she said. "It was just beautiful."

One of the similarities of the courses, although unbeknownst to some of the participants at the time, is the hilly terrain. "Somebody said it was hilly," quipped Meyer of the Ohme-Hochi 30K. "And it was!"

Ome mayor Toshio Takeuchi (*center*) presents 2015 Boston Marathon winners Caroline Rotich of Kenya (*left*) and Lelisa Desisa of Ethiopia with customary gifts from Japan. *Photo by Paul Clerici.*

In 2015, BAA president Joann Flamino signs the Boston Marathon/Ohme-Hochi 30K Athlete Exchange Program extension agreement with Ome mayor Toshio Takeuchi (*right*). *Photo by Paul Clerici.*

Amako agreed with that sentiment—but for the Boston Marathon. "I didn't know and I didn't realize that there were going to be so many hills up and down," she smiled.

Hasegawa, who also was unaware of the hills, simply focused on the Boston Marathon as a whole once he was selected due to his 2015 Ohme-Hochi 30K win.

"Once I found out I was coming, I trained all through the winter and I look forward to the Boston Marathon," he said. "That's all I really thought of. I wanted to do my personal best in Boston and I was able to do that. [In Boston] we did course inspection a couple of days before and I had no idea there were going to be so many hills."

Like with most non-elite athletes, the excitement alone of the Boston Marathon can get the adrenaline going. It is no different for the elite as well, even though it is their job.

"I was so excited from the beginning that I think I went out too fast from the very beginning and I realize that halfway through and it was pretty tough on my body," recalled Hasegawa. "Heartbreak Hill completely wrecked my knees and legs. [Ohme] is a there-and-back [course, but] in my mind it is kind of similar—it is uphill [the first half] and the back is downhill. When I ran Ohme [in 2015], I did negative split. But [in Boston], I did not do that," he laughed.

Another challenge for visitors can be food. Japanese delicacies include the likes of fish, sushi, rice, spices, soups, octopus, pork belly, jellyfish, and even barnacles.

"Food is my biggest indulgence," Arciniaga acknowledged. "The hotel we were staying in had eggs, bacon—traditional American breakfast. But whenever I do travel, I try to sample and try out food wherever I am. Culture's food, so it's not something that's new to me."

And even though the Ohme-Hochi 30K was canceled in 1996, 2008, and 2014 due to heavy snow and 2021 and 2022 due to COVID-19 restrictions, as was the Boston Marathon as an in-person race in 2020 due to the pandemic, there seems no end in sight for this unique exchange of athletes and culture.

"We are very proud of our relationship with BAA," said Otake via Honda. "Having exchange program to send officials and athletes every year—with BAA [and] one of world oldest marathon race—athletes are very proud of participating [in the] race. Every five years both parties extend agreement, and hoping this good relation will continue for ever."

Morse reinforces that notion.

"[It's] predicated with the complete understanding that this will continue on forever, whatever forever is," he said. "When it started—and in its younger years—it was pretty rare. These exchanges didn't happen. It wasn't a 40-year agreement or a 100-year agreement [at first, but] in theory it probably will be."

5

ATHLETE VILLAGES

When it comes to handling participants at the Boston Marathon, it actually takes more than a village, it takes two—the Boston Marathon Elite Athletes' Village (EAV) and the separate non-elite Boston Marathon Athletes' Village (AV), which combined are designed to embrace the entire field.

In 1996, when the Boston Athletic Association (BAA) increased the entrant total to 38,708 for the race's centennial celebration (the previous peak was 9,629 entrants in 1992), the AV was set up in Hopkinton, at the sports fields behind the high school and middle school. It is where the non-elite athletes congregate in the hours before the race each Patriots' Day morning.

For the professional elite athletes, it was shortly after the race's first principal sponsorship began in 1986 with John Hancock Mutual Life Insurance Company that the EAV was created to accommodate the invited Olympians, Paralympians, national champions, record-setters, and marathon winners.

For the 2012 race, the John Hancock Boston Marathon EAV moved to the 1912 historic seven-floor, 383-room Fairmont Copley Plaza Hotel, which also hosts the world media and various press conferences and events. Led by Mary Kate Shea, BAA director of professional athletes, parts of two floors are dedicated housing for the pro elite athletes, along with supplemental rooms for hospitality services, food, media, and more. It requires a thorough process to gather together such an impressive field each year.

"You must be one of the fastest marathon runners in the world, bring championship experience to the race, and represent your country and the sport to the highest degree. I seek highly motivated runners who may have a win/loss history with each other and then mix in upcoming elites who want to prove they belong on a major stage. Racing well without pacesetters and on challenging courses is also a plus. Strength on hills and smart racing is a must," Shea explained. "There is a lot of research and communication involved in putting together the field. I work mostly with World Athletics-certified agent representatives from around the globe and in some cases the athletes themselves to secure race participation. We have a great internal team who set up a world-class experience for the [elites]—from arranging flights, transportation, hospitality, course tours, course training, lodging, communal dining, and more. Our communications, creative and marketing/brand teams, all work together to tell the story of these amazing athletes."

The original John Hancock EAV—from 1989 to 2011—was housed in the nearby eight-story, 64-room John Hancock Hotel and Conference Center, in the shadow of the iconic 60-story glass former John Hancock Tower, just blocks from the finish line. Razed in 2020, when the John Hancock Hotel and Conference Center was the Boston Common Hotel and Conference Center, the unassuming-looking 18th-century Adam-style brick exterior hid the fact it served as a two-week home and security fortress for on average

Boston Marathon Athletes' Village in Hopkinton. *Photo by Paul Clerici.*

100 combined staff, 90 guests, 40 hosts, 30-plus elite athletes, 20 agents, and a half-dozen coaches.

For those entrusted each year with the occupants' well-being at the old hotel and conference center, the heart of the building was three rooms on the third floor: the Boiler Room, Athlete Processing Room, and Host Workroom.

The Boiler Room of computers and files contained all the vital information on each athlete, including arrival and departure times, entourage lists, appearance schedules, food and medical requirements, training and religious necessities, assigned living quarter lists, and anything else involved in their safety and comfort while staying in Boston. Details also included whatever assistance that may be required in relation to visas, passports, tax forms, and applications.

"It's all here," noted global sports and event management firm TRACS Inc. founder, president, and CEO Fred Treseler, former director of the original setup, in 2009. "We sit down and do all their tax forms with them and their prize-money forms. And they have to sign their race application and an information sheet. Forms and schedules were also sent to their agents a month out to share with their athletes. So they know what's going on in case they want to set up something with their shoe company, for example—they'll know about their commitments. We also send them a copy of the menu in case they have any dietary requests because we can handle that as well."

A record 36,748 starters at the first Boston Marathon Athletes' Village in Hopkinton for the 1996 centennial. *Photo by Paul Clerici.*

Nothing is deemed too small of importance.

"We coordinate with the catering service, we coordinate with the limousine company, we coordinate with the management of the hotel and conference center and the other hotels where some of the athletes stay, we work on flight-departure confirmations when they arrive," Treseler listed. "We also have their actual water bottles and bib numbers and the forms they will turn in with their water bottles for the race. It's pretty extensive."

Early on, to accommodate all this data and scheduling, and to ensure its safety and applicability, a customized computer software system was created by Treseler's son, Freddie Tressler IV (TRACS senior account manager), and Lisa Plesko (former TRACS program director for emerging elites), both of whom also created a complementary website that agents could access for immediate information, schedules, and requests.

"If we need to generate a report, like a race-day credential report, we can instantly call up these types of reports and we can tell that these official staff passes have been issued for race day and here are all the numbers on the back of the passes," Treseler explained. "We set up a very clean, systematic operation."

For example, with athletes departing from anywhere in the United States on airlines such as Alaska, America, and United or from other countries on airlines including Air France, KLM Royal Dutch, and Lufthansa, schedules and logistics can get convoluted if not for a streamlined system.

"We built this from the ground up," said Treseler IV, of the nascent computer system from the early days. "We had 12 different tables on the old system and now we have two. On this system, we can sort flights, arrivals— international, domestic—on a specific date, gates, and even all the agents. We have 17 agents for 29 athletes and over 200 flights—in and out– because people are coming from different locations at different times."

For the original and the new EAV, similar organizational meetings begin in January, and the actual EAV setup takes up to a week or two before it opens for the athletes. Everything must adhere to a tight schedule because arrivals are not dependent on completion of the setup. People will appear regardless of whether the computer lines, race banners, or buffet tables are ready. In 2009, for instance, Easter Sunday occurred the week before the Marathon, and the staff and volunteers still came to work throughout the day because that Sunday is always a busy one despite being eight days ahead Patriots' Day.

"For the people that manage this whole thing, it's a real act of love. They don't get a ton of interaction with the athletes," noted Treseler, in regard to the original EAV. "This is all the strength and the business power of making this all run behind the scenes. Like any major sporting event, you need to have tremendous volunteers behind the organization. We are very, very blessed. Quite often it takes two, three, four, or five volunteers per participant. [And] after we get all the computers and tables and things set up, we also dress up the building so it looks like an athletic venue in carrying the brand of the sponsor and the image of the event. And we have training sessions, too, for the volunteers and the hosts."

Boston Marathon race director Dave McGillivray, also a runner, understands the needs and requirements of both the athletes and the organizers.

"The intent is to try to provide an environment—particularly for the elite athletes who do this for a living and take it obviously real seriously; and they only have one or two of these in them a year—to give them an opportunity to relax, eat properly, and to just be in an environment where come race day they'll be able to perform to the highest level. We recognize that, and we want to take it to the nth degree. I think we do that here. Other races do it [to an extent], but I think we do it as well as anybody," he said. "The whole idea is that all their energy goes into when the gun fires, not before the gun fires. And it benefits us for them to run well, too. One may look at it as being an unselfish thing on our part to provide that opportunity to them. But in reality, it's also selfish, but in a positive manner because we, too, want them to perform extremely well. It makes all of us look good."

U.S. Olympian Brian Sell, who at Boston was 4th in 2006 and 14th in 2009, found no comparison in regard to the provided hospitality services in Boston.

"It's second to none. They take care of us. They tell us where to be [and] when. They provide the meals and everything," he observed about the original EAV. "The rooms are nice—they're quiet and they're kind of away from the epicenter of everything. It just works out really great. [In 2009] I honestly felt a little guilty because I had five [Hansons-Brooks Distance Project] teammates that weren't in the Hancock program and I always felt bad because they're the guys that were out there running the same miles and workouts that I was, but I got a little extra better treatment than they did. But I'll take it when I can get it."

The journey begins for most of the elite athletes just four miles northeast of the EAV, at Logan International Airport, in East Boston. Waiting for the approximate 40 domestic and international arrivals is a continuous stream of about a dozen drivers and 40 hosts who on a regular basis of nearly 165 trips greet and pick up participants, coaches, agents, physicians, family members—anyone associated with the athletes whose involvement provides any kind of comfort during their time in Boston.

Operations overseer Fred Treseler, TRACS president and CEO, in 2009, at the Boston Marathon Elite Athletes' Village inside the John Hancock Hotel and Conference Center at Trinity Place. *Photo by Paul Clerici.*

"We have large boards in the Boiler Room and the Hosts Room that list the names of all the runners, their airlines, flights, arrivals, gates, and the hosts and their cell phone numbers," explained Treseler of the original EAV. "We send out a driver and a host. And the host is responsible if there are any delays or side trips, not the driver—the driver drives. Our host's job is to make the connection, even if an athlete wants to go shopping. The host will reconnect with the driver."

Based on the information on the boards, a host will know when, where, and whom to pick up. The board also lists any children who would require a child seat in the limo and any other pertinent details.

"Also on the board are flower symbols for the women athletes that are coming in and we take flowers to them when the hosts go to the airport," said former veteran host Pat Lodigiani, in 2009, of the personal touch. "The host has a laminated sign with the individual's name on it—because [the athlete is] expecting someone to meet them—and the hosts also have a packet of material for the athlete. And there are two different times [listed] next to an athlete's name on the board: the time that the flight is expected and the time we send the host so they have enough time to get to the airport, check in through airport security—which is new—and get to the terminal where the athlete is expecting us to be."

Upon welcoming elite athletes, hosts tend to the luggage, accompany visitors to the vehicle, and report in that the connection has been made and that they are soon returning. Calls ensure there are no questions regarding airport pickups.

"We're in constant contact," said Lodigiani. "We had an occasion when an athlete brought their own physical therapist who was not on the list. The host is instructed not to bring anybody unless they're on the list, so that host called us from the airport. Everything is checked because of the security issue. And because we are a curious society," she added with a smile, "hosts do not answer any questions on who they're meeting, where they're going to stay, or any of that information because you never know who's asking and it's [also] basically no one else's business. Also, when they're about five minutes away, the host calls so we can get our processing people ready for when they arrive."

All arrivals, delays, changes, and eventual departures are constantly monitored and checked. The goal is to be proactive and to anticipate. If there is a flight delay, for example, the driver and host endeavor to be there before the athlete, not the other way around. A worst-case scenario would be to have a foreign, non–English speaking elite athlete seeking direction in one of the busiest airports in the country.

When things go smoothly, athletes then arrive at the EAV less than 20 minutes after they depart Logan. At the original EAV, their quarters were closed to the public while the athletes were there, and the entrance was from where, on race day, they left on comfortable coach buses to the start in Hopkinton.

Two-time U.S. Olympian Elva Dryer, 12th at the 2009 Boston, was particularly grateful for the hospitality services she received prior to that year's race.

"Eliminating any chaos or any type of thing that you might come across, like when my flight was delayed and we came in late. I just called my agent to let him know to let whoever know [in Boston] that my flight was late. And somebody was there [waiting at Logan]. They stayed up," she recalled. "Perhaps at another race I'd have to find my way—not always, but at some races. So it's nice to have someone there to guide you along the way."

At other races, there are times when no one will be waiting for a pro athlete at the airport.

"[At] some marathons, you have to get your own cab from the airport. But generally, you get reimbursed," noted Sell. "But this was nice [in

One of the many responsibilities at the Boston Marathon Elite Athletes' Village in the John Hancock Hotel and Conference Center at Trinity Place was tracking all athlete and guest airline arrivals and departures, as monitored by Stacie Finnegan (*left*) and Steve Peckiconis. *Photo by Paul Clerici.*

Boston]. As soon as I got off the airplane, there's a guy waiting with my name on the board. I hopped in a big Chevy Suburban, all leather and everything, and I felt like a celebrity. It's definitely a step above what most other races do, for sure."

Four-time New Zealand Olympian and 1984 Boston winner Lorraine Moller, who won Marathon bronze at the 1992 Barcelona Olympic Games, has experienced marathon accommodations at both ends of the spectrum.

"In Boston, I was always treated very well. The hospitality was wonderful. I started to get used to that. It was very nice. It was like being royalty," she said. "But my first marathon, in Minnesota, I went with my boyfriend and we drove up the night before and I wasn't even entered. We ended up knocking on the door of the race director after some frantic phone calls and picking up a number at 10 o'clock the night before. It was a lot more low-level than what I got introduced to later on. Once I started going to the Avon marathons, and there was a lot more money behind it, it was like heaven. When you got a free hotel room and somebody paid your airfare, it was like we were made."

Upon entering the original EAV after their airport trip, still accompanied by their hosts, athletes were directed to the Athlete Processing Room, where registration took place, credentials were issued, and any questions answered.

"The building is locked at night, so all of our guests, all of our staff, and all of the athletes get a specific credential that John Hancock security created for us," said Treseler, in 2009, of the original EAV procedure. "The credential gets you in through the front doors, and then you go to security, so there's a double layer of security there."

At registration, athletes could also inquire about and sign up for course tours—which were originally guided by the late USATF National Track & Field Hall of Fame coach Bill Squires—transportation requests, tourist sites, and massages, all of which were funneled through the Boiler Room.

"It's quite a setup for the athletes," noted Bill Morris, who was lead massage therapist and head of the medical and massage area of the original EAV. "One of the interesting things here is that you've got guys and gals that have come off 16, 18 weeks of training in altitude, and most coaches will put them on the track two weeks before [the Boston Marathon]. And I can tell you the number of elite athletes who have needed me to work on their feet. They're 100 percent fit going straight, but going on a track—the knees, hips, feet! I've had guys that have been crippled after a week and a half, but you keep working on them every day and see how their runs go. The next thing you know, you see the guy winning. Doesn't happen all the time. But it's neat. And one of the keys to the dining hall is I get to see everybody walk in and walk out, and I can see gaits, I can see limps, especially if I've worked with an athlete before. It's really a valuable experience for me."

Occupying a large conference meeting room and stage on the second floor of the original setup was that dining hall, with dozens of round tables dressed with tablecloths, cheerful centerpieces, bottles of sports drinks, race banners and other race-related signage, buffets, a large video screen that showed the course and previous races, and plenty of race talk in a variety of languages and dialects.

"They do a phenomenal job, from the color scheme to the setup, and, of course, the catering," Treseler pointed out, in 2009. "On the Sunday before the race we'll feed over 300 people. And with the food, everything is labeled. But they also in some instances put pictures with the food. For example, in the morning if there's turkey or pork sausages, they'll have a picture of a turkey or a pig so any religious concerns are addressed. And we've refined the menu over many, many years."

Located near the dining hall, a stadium-seating conference room doubled as a hotbed of nonrunning sports activities for the athletes, thanks in large part to Squires, when he wasn't conducting the course tours or answering questions about the course he knew so well. For relaxation and fun, the most popular game for the elite athletes was the every-expanding miniature golf course, where participants putt a golf ball from the conference room, out the door to the hallway, down the stairs via plastic tubing, through the ground-floor lobby, into the elevator, and to wherever else Squires had designed the course.

In the Hosts Room, volunteer hosts began their day by checking in for their shift and responsibilities, which included any number of athlete assignments such as airport trips, press conferences, public appearances, training locations, and tourist excursions. Hosts also referred to a separate board that featured a color copy of each athlete's credentials, picture, and name, to ensure proper connections.

"We have a good system working where they even learn about their airport runs a day or two in advance. In case they're tied up at work, they know they can call in and make plans," Treseler explained. "We even have flashcards, like you had in school, where hosts can learn all about the athletes' names, which are on the back of the photos. They have a contest

Nerve center of the Boston Marathon Elite Athletes' Village, called the Boiler Room, inside the John Hancock Hotel and Conference Center at Trinity Place, in 2009. *Photo by Paul Clerici.*

at night, trying to figure out who can out-flashcard the others. We kind of make it fun."

Hosts also ensure each individual room is ready, which included flowers in each female athlete's room, a course description on every nightstand, and showing athletes how to work the thermostat so they can adjust the room to their personal preference, since the athletes live in different climates around the world.

"This one's certainly in a league of its own as far as hospitality and just seeing that every athlete's needs are met. Everything's so convenient," said Dryer, a five-time U.S. national champion, of the original EAV. "Basically, you just tell them what you need and somehow they come through. It's one less thing to think about when you have to get ready for an event like this. Even dealing with the little stuff like getting a refrigerator in my room because my husband's insulin dependent, I just made a phone call and it showed up. And having water on each floor—you just have to walk out of your door and there it is. Having a schedule—letting you know where to be at a certain time, rather than having to search for that information; having people guiding you through the whole process—for somebody like me, I like that. And I'm even a bit of a control freak."

Ryan Hall, 2008 U.S. Olympic Marathon Trials winner who was third at the 2009 Boston, treasured the accommodations of the original EAV during his stay.

"It's huge. It allows you to basically have a home in Boston, which is always the best environment to run out of," he said. "That's why back home is such a powerful place because it's where you get your nutrients from, it's where you get your power from. So to have a safe haven in Boston—and not get hounded all the time and be able to relax; and it's quiet; the food is good, it's healthy, it's right there and it's easy—it gives you the opportunity to be at the highest level that you possibly can."

The third floor of the original EAV, which included no sleeping quarters, housed the private enclosed massage room and a makeshift lobby that featured healthy snacks, fruit, and even an ice cream and yogurt machine; a living-room-style place to read or watch television or videos of previous races; and smaller conference rooms in which to meet coaches, agents, or visitors.

"These are places outside their room where they can relax," said Treseler. "It's a place where they don't have to deal with the public or the press. They're in a secured area. And no matter when people come in during the day or night, and if they're a little bit out of cycle with their dietary situation, there is always something available for them."

For a runner as high profile and in demand as was Hall, the seclusion was welcome.

"It's great to interact with the people and the thousands that will be out there running, but you just have to do it at the right time," he noted. "So every time you go to your room, to have it take 20 minutes to go through the hotel lobby can be exhausting sometimes [at other venues]. That's what's so nice about the John Hancock Center."

At the original EAV, anytime athletes or someone with them requested transportation to a press conference or public appearance or for a personal matter, it was coordinated through the Boiler Room to the Transportation Office inside the front of the building, between the front door and security.

"Anything that has to do with moving the athletes or staff through John Hancock, we do it through this office," noted Marc Schpilner, contractor for transportation. "When the host comes down from upstairs to get them at the airport, we do all the flight checks, we get the hosts to the airport, we get them situated at the airport, we get them checked in properly with a greeter pass to walk into the terminal. We then meet them [hosts and guests] curbside, load them in, and bring them back to the facility."

Most days every vehicle could be in use at the same time, especially when course tours, press conferences, public appearances, and shopping visits either coincided or partially overlapped.

"They've done a very good job in centralizing requests through one desk," said Schpilner. "We've kind of centralized it over the years to flow through one location filtered down to us. There could be a hundred different scenarios that could go wrong—no host, no vehicle, an athlete was supposed to be at a press conference and they decided to go shopping. They've done a really good job monitoring and managing how the athletes are moved."

Prior to such elite athlete door-to-door service, when 1974 Boston winner and two-time Irish Olympian Neil Cusack traveled to the Hub that year, he arrived with less assistance and fanfare.

"I came up from East Tennessee State University with a friend of mine and I stayed at their house for about three days where I trained," recalled Cusack, an ETSU Buccaneer at the time. "I came to Boston the night before and I stayed at a hotel. It was just me. I got up the next morning about six o'clock and ran about two miles—you're always freer the second run of the day. I had the usual toast and something light, and then I got the bus out to Hopkinton—one of the yellow [school] buses!

Stayed in the gym and just limbered up, got ready, and we were called down to the start line."

The overall design of the original EAV, especially the third floor, grew organically through Treseler's firm, which, he said, was involved from the very beginning of John Hancock's sponsorship. TRACS was originally hired to create for schools a national running and fitness program that featured athletes under contract with John Hancock to run Boston. Within the first dozen or so years, they visited more than 90,000 schoolchildren in 32 states.

"We took the athletes into middle schools, grammar schools, and high schools, and we did different activities with the students to promote running and fitness," Treseler explained. "And after the 1988 Boston Marathon, we were asked to take over the hospitality part of the event on behalf of John Hancock."

Most major-city marathons feature a host hotel in which the elite-athlete hospitality services are housed. The hotel also usually is the location for the bib number pickup, runner expo, and pre-race pasta dinner for all the participants (elite and non-elite), along with the hotel's other unrelated events. It is not uncommon to walk into a race host hotel and see pro athletes and amateur marathoners among people who are attending computer or physician conventions at the same time.

"We were lucky to discover this building existed," said Treseler in 2009, of the since-razed John Hancock Hotel and Conference Center. "We were very

Boston Marathon Athletes' Village entrance in Hopkinton. *Photo by Paul Clerici.*

blessed that John Hancock [owned] this building two blocks from the finish line and it has hotel space and wonderful meeting space. Initially, we didn't use all of the space. It really evolved since 1989."

It boggles the mind at how the original EAV evolved over its 23 years.

"This is a lot of fun for everybody because it's very, very different," said Treseler in 2009. "This is just a different setup. There's no place, to my knowledge, that does it anywhere like this. We were asked to get involved with this component to try to make it the best in the world."

Added Sell about the hospitality services, "It's very important before a big marathon. We train three, four months and this is it. We don't have another race next week to go out and redeem ourselves if we have a bad one here. It's very important. I think all the runners really appreciate having that all set up and done for us already. It makes our job that much easier—to just focus on the race and not worry about anything else."

6

EVOLUTION OF MEDIA COVERAGE

The Boston Marathon has always drawn enough interest to be covered in the media. Since 1897, newspapers, sports cartoonists, photographers, radio, newsreels, television, magazines, books, digital channels, blogs, and more have all featured the race in one form or another. And with this interest, and an ever-growing stream of media outlets, the Boston Athletic Association (BAA) over the decades has expanded and evolved its infrastructure and accommodations for those who report on and cover the race.

"Because of the interest in this event—and it's unlike any other—there's more media that cover the Boston Marathon than any other [running] event," noted BAA Board of Governor and former Boston Marathon race director Guy Morse III. "It's actually the largest single-day sporting event for media credentials in the world, annually, except for the Super Bowl" (with reportedly more than 1,300 media passes representing over 250 outlets for the race).

In the beginning, runners were approached by reporters and photographers quite liberally, and sometimes at their homes or workplaces, for interviews and stories. Then came cinema newsreels and TV, both of which introduced the moving visual aspect of the sport. But it was limited in the early days, as footage was extremely minimal. Even 70 years in, with no wire-to-wire coverage, Ambrose "Amby" Burfoot did not benefit when he won in 1968.

"I don't remember any video coverage, honestly. It certainly was not national or anything like that," he recalled. "I do know they [the BAA, when Burfoot was honored at a reception] couldn't find any video of me running. I think I provided six seconds that we had stolen from a cable station or something like that. But there was not a lot of video. Certainly not easy to find."

Four-time Boston Marathon and four-time New York City Marathon winner Bill Rodgers also recalls the lack of coverage from his viewpoint of seeing vehicles in front of him as he competed.

"When I won New York, it wasn't covered by national TV. It wasn't on TV in the '70s. In '79, I think there was one camera at the finish or something," he said. "In Boston, they'd have a media truck and they had cameras, I think, stationed at certain points along the course [but not live start-to-finish coverage]."

Ground-level sourcing and gathering of information, from where it all begins in terms of telling the stories, has certainly experienced quantum leaps. For decades, Boston Marathon checkpoints (time splits of which were also available to the media) coincided with train stops where officials deboarded and reboarded the train en route to the finish, as the road and tracks parallel each other for part of the course. By the time award-

An example of early press coverage of the Boston Marathon with three-time winner Leslie "Les" Pawson (1933, 1938, 1941) being filmed, circa 1940. *Courtesy of the Boston Public Library, Leslie Jones Collection.*

winning Running USA Hall of Champion race broadcaster Toni Reavis first covered Boston in 1977, along the course were "spotters" who sent back information via pay phones or other devices. "It just evolved from there," he pointed out.

To gather race-day info for the record and the media, Boston uses a multisource system of communication from officials on bicycles and lead vehicles on the course, as well as BAA media volunteers, television production personnel, and additional chip mats for more precise data.

However, when women's running pioneer Kathrine Switzer—1974 New York City winner and six-time top-five Boston finisher—first covered Boston in 1979 for WGBH-TV, Boston's Public Broadcasting Service (PBS) station, data collection was archaic in comparison. Early PBS coverage was considered sophisticated in its complexity and (delayed) delivery, despite the arduous physicality of delivering videotapes of the race to the TV studio for airing.

"The first two years that I did the broadcast, it was the first time that it had been broadcast nationally—nationwide that night," she noted of

Boston Herald-Traveler newspaper photographer Leslie Ronald Jones (*standing*) at the BAA press vehicle in 1938. *Courtesy of the Boston Public Library, Leslie Jones Collection.*

the tape delay. "We did it off of battery-powered golf carts, and the carts couldn't even make it up the hills. We had these great big three-quarter-inch tapes [of the race] and we would come alongside at these points [along the course] and we'd throw it over the crowd. And there's a guy on a bike and he would motorbike it back to WGBH and they were racking them up and editing the show as we were commentating. And then we went into the show [afterward] and closed it live. It was unbelievable!"

And all too often the monitors were unclear, which made it difficult to describe the race.

"When we started going live, there was so much [visual] breakup, and the monitors were never good. It was always very fuzzy stuff," recalled Switzer. "As a runner, you identify people by their walk and their run—their body type—long before you can see their face. You just don't lose that technique. So that's how we'd have to call the race often because we couldn't see the numbers, couldn't see their faces or anything. We'd just call by body type. I remember calling the [Alberto] Salazar-[Dick] Beardsley race [in 1982]. Couldn't even see their numbers or face, but we knew, of course, who they were. You could tell what was happening just because of their body type."

In 1975, early technology first included the Runner Administration and Computerized Entry Routines (RACER) computer software system by Honeywell, which in 1980 added barcodes on the bib numbers to expedite results. Finishers lined up in the chutes, and one by one volunteers recorded each barcode, which enabled RACER to tabulate and print results for the media and participants.

To increase overall accuracy for the media, the Spotters Network was formed of official volunteers stationed throughout the course. Via coach Fred Treseler's global sports and event management firm TRACS Inc.'s Race SpotWatch division—created by Treseler and former Boston Marathon race director Tim Kilduff—the 100-plus-strong group was trained how to watch, record, and communicate time splits and other race-related information in real time.

"The Spotters Network [in later years exists] in a different form than it did then," Morse said of the program, which started in 1985. "From those [early] days when everything was recorded, at best, over a hardline telephone that might have been there—or radio, walkie-talkie, even at the official checkpoints—the officials would write down the bib numbers and the times and they'd be brought to the finish line, physically, and tabulated there. There was always a huge time delay. But of course, no one knew any different in those days. That was the norm."

WBZ-TV of Boston has covered the Marathon since 1981. Emmy Award–winning television journalist Lisa Hughes, who has reported from the lead women's press truck, the course, the finish, and the media bridge as anchor of its live wire-to-wire programming, uses everything the BAA and the Spotters Network provide.

"Our goal was to produce an exciting, entertaining program that highlighted great competition and the pride in the event that connects us," she said. "We introduced viewers to elite runners through stories and interviews before the race and used every technology at our disposal to provide the best race coverage. Adding multiple 'boxes' so that viewers could watch races simultaneously was an important addition. We kept our coverage of the races going during the commercial breaks in those boxes. Our reporters were placed, strategically, along the course. The Spotters Network were our 'eyes on the ground' in areas where we didn't have WBZ reporters. Our coverage changed as technology changed. But we always relied on our 'people power' most of all—the skills of our reporters, photographers, and members of the Spotters Network. While the elite/professional runners were our main focus in the first half of race day, we made an effort—every year—to improve our coverage of the charity runners."

In the early 1980s, what became known in Boston as the TV Wars, emerged from competition between the "big three" affiliates of ABC (WCVB-TV), CBS (WHDH-TV), and NBC (WBZ-TV). While all local stations featured some kind of programming, WBZ-TV (NBC until 1995, CBS since 1996) was first to program start-to-finish coverage in 1981, followed by WCVB-TV in 1982, and then WHDH-TV. Over time, WHDH-TV stopped its wire-to-wire coverage in the mid-1990s, followed by WCVB-TV in 2006, and then WBZ-TV's ended in 2022.

It's all about providing the best coverage possible to the widest audience. WBZ-TV, which held the exclusive wire-to-wire broadcast rights from 2007 to 2022, reported its highest viewer numbers of 494,200 in 2014, when American Meb Keflezighi won Boston the year following the 2013 bombings.

"Calling his 2014 Boston Marathon victory—live—is one of the highlights of my career," noted Hughes. "After the painful year we'd all endured after the Marathon bombing, his win was the crowning moment on a joyous day."

Added Mark Lund, former WBZ-TV president and general manager, in 2014, "The day was spectacular, the champions were truly extraordinary, the runners were all winners in their own ways, and the community celebrated resilience and triumph. Everyone at WBZ work[ed] on bringing the Boston

With increased viewership and outlets, media vans line up along the streets of Hopkinton Town Common during the week of the Boston Marathon. *Photo by Paul Clerici.*

Marathon to the community and we are so gratified that so many people tuned in to 'BZ to celebrate this historic race."

To broaden its reach, the BAA in 2023 signed WCVB-TV/ESPN as exclusive local/national broadcast partners. The new agreement ensures all BAA races and events will enjoy local television exposure throughout the year.

"We're honored to partner with ESPN and WCVB Channel 5, respected market leaders who bring a spirit of innovation and thoughtful storytelling that will propel the mission of the BAA and legacy of the world's oldest annual marathon forward," said BAA CEO and president Jack Fleming.

The new deal returns wire-to-wire programming to WCVB-TV after a seventeen-year absence.

"The BAA and the Boston Marathon are esteemed around the world and beloved by our community, and to be launching this exclusive partnership as WCVB marks 50 years in broadcasting and service to the community is especially fitting," stated WCVB-TV president and general manager Kyle Grimes.

ESPN covered the Boston Marathon in the 1980s and for eight years from 1997 to 2004.

"The Boston Marathon is one of the world's most recognizable and best-known sporting events and we're proud to be able to bring it to ESPN viewers for years to come," stated ESPN president of programming and original content Burke Magnus.

Having a single station also enables the BAA to streamline the media vehicles on the course. Before the days of pool coverage—multiple media outlets using coverage from one camera source—it was a crowded course.

"Before it became really coordinated, there were competing stations with competing vehicles on the course, so there were way too many vehicles on the course," noted Morse. "Each entity in the old days did their own thing and that became dangerous. It really wasn't an issue in the sport because most other races didn't have that number of people covering it, television-wise or otherwise. But we did here. So at some point—say there were three or four networks all with their own vehicles—it became very dangerous and congested and then everyone suffered because it wasn't good-quality video."

Early attempts to accommodate the press corps included the use of makeshift vehicles, often commercial buses, which themselves at times also affected the athletes.

In front of the world media, Boston Marathon media conferences include interviews and photo ops. *Photo by Paul Clerici.*

"I remember the press bus, as they called it, was actually, one year, a bus with 45 press on it, hanging out the windows, backwards, to see what's going on," Morse recalled. "Imagine a lumbering bus in front of the course, blowing black smoke and the whole bit."

As interest and coverage grew, so did the need for informed and knowledgeable staff and on-air personnel to properly convey the sport. Too many instances occurred with the unappreciated aspect of coverage of commentators and reporters who simply did not understand.

"The difference between respect and disrespect was knowledge of what we were doing and empathy with what we were doing," said the late 1957 Boston winner Johnny "The Younger" Kelley. "Those guys like [*Boston Globe* sports editor] Jerry Nason were knowledgeable and empathetic. There were others that I could name who were not knowledgeable and didn't want to be knowledgeable, and their shtick was really being unempathetic."

After Rodgers won the 1975 Boston with an American record, he was interviewed on a radio show and subject to that very disrespect.

"I just set the American record—it was the fastest time in the world that year—and I went on a local radio show and this very well-known sports guy said, literally said to my face, 'Well, you're not an athlete,' because I didn't throw a ball or something like that. I threw a few here and there, now come on," he recalled with a laugh. "But you know what I'm saying. I think it was because it was an amateur sport and it was kind of below the line of vision in a certain sense, communication-wise. The media always knew about Boston because there weren't a lot of marathons then. This race had been around so long that when you heard the name marathon, it was the Boston Marathon, so the media paid attention to it. But they didn't understand it athletically, I don't think."

Switzer was aware of the issue and always made a point to spend time with journalists who might not fully grasp the sport. As an activist, organizer, commentator, and especially a runner, she also brings with her the unique perspective of a female athlete in the once male-dominated arena.

"I felt very, very sorry for a lot of reporters because clearly—you know, every time we ran a marathon, and we did it, and we were running better than anybody could ever imagine—they were lacking knowledge," she said. "So I pride myself in taking an enormous amount of time, sitting down and explaining the rationale, and what my feelings were."

Not all early commentators were bad, of course. Some at the beginning understood running and appreciated its value.

"There are always wonderful people, special people, who are great commentators who know the names and they were good from the beginning on," noted three-time Boston winner Uta Pippig. "But I think more and more people are aware of the sport, and more and more people know [enough] to talk about it and to feel what's going on out there in the field, to see what's going on, and also to know the background."

Two-time U.S. Olympian and two-time top-five Boston finisher Alan Culpepper appreciates the fact that knowledge in road-racing coverage has improved.

"A marathon is kind of its own deal [and it's] nice to have people who understand what you're doing and understand what you're trying to accomplish," he said. "Especially surrounding this type of race—a marathon."

One way to fill that knowledge gap is to provide the viewing audience with commentators who are runners. As evident from the Hall of Fame lineups on TV for the Boston Marathon, this influx of former and current runners is a major boost.

"It is an easy transition," noted Pippig, who did make that move from runner to commentator. "Unfortunately for me, it was a little bit of a language barrier because I obviously came from East Germany, and from Germany—language-wise, it was tough. Sometimes the picture was going so fast and I had all my ideas and the picture was gone and obviously you can't talk about it anymore. One major thing is there is a huge amount of work behind TV coverage production—research; the whole technique; all the cameras along the way; the leading vehicle; to have people on the press truck; and to coordinate us all in the studio. Maybe one advantage we [runners] have compared to, let's say [as] a sportscaster, [is] when you come from running you can tell a story behind the scene. You can sneak into the runner's mind. You can feel what's going on for the runner who's out there. So you cannot just see the picture, you can feel the picture, too. And it comes natural. You don't have to think about it."

Two-time Boston champion Joan Benoit Samuelson, who began her on-air race commentator experience in the 1980s, possesses a unique perspective in front of the camera—from the road and the broadcasting booth—as to how her sport has evolved.

"I think it's very similar [now], with the exception of the first time I ran Boston," she said. "Nobody knew who I was and I just sort of came down the night before, slept with some friends [at their house], got up and went to the starting line. I wasn't prepared to deal with the onslaught of the press afterward, nor did I know the course. So ignorance is bliss that way. Now it's pretty standard. The press conferences the couple of days before the event; all the psyche that the runners go through; all the psychological preparations the runners go through; the press discussing the players, the day, the weather."

When stations realized the advantage of sport-specific commentators— moving on from non-marathon notables, as when national network journalist Katie Couric, U.S. Olympic gold-medal speedskater Dan Jansen, and national network news anchor Matt Lauer were featured in Boston Marathon TV coverage—over the years it became a who's who of the running world who joined the regular anchors. The list included the likes of eight-time Boston wheelchair winner Jean Driscoll, U.S. Olympic 10,000-meter silver medalist Shalane Flanagan, U.S. Olympic Marathon bronze medalist Deena Kastor, Kilduff, Pippig, Reavis, Rodgers, Samuelson, U.S. Olympic Marathon gold and silver medalist Frank Shorter, USATF National Track & Field Hall of Fame coach Bill Squires, Switzer, and Norway Olympic Marathon silver medalist Grete Waitz among them.

National cable stations such as ESPN, Outdoor Life Network (OLN), SportsChannel, Versus, and others also took notice and featured their own stars, which have included award-winning sports broadcaster Al Trautwig, Emmy Award–winning race commentator Larry Rawson, two-time U.S. Olympic High Jump silver medalist Dwight Stones, and 1,500-meter U.S. Olympian Carrie Tollefson, among others.

"We thought for our first year covering the event [in 2005], our telecast went very smoothly thanks to our experienced programming and production team working in conjunction with Clear Channel and the BAA," stated former OLN senior vice president of programming and production Marc Fein. "Between the three of us, we had the proper personnel and knowledge to pull it off. Luckily, there were no major obstacles to overcome."

When John Hancock Mutual Life Insurance Company in 1986 became the first principal sponsor of the race, the course changed, the finish line moved, the field swelled, prize money was awarded, the number of international elite athletes grew, and the world media followed.

"We didn't change the nature or the spirit of the event, but we did take it to a new level in terms of corporate support, which led to prize money and a much better media operations support for the press," Morse noted. "So it was in the mid-'80s when it really took off in terms of coverage and press. It was pretty quick. It was always covered internationally—it used to be called the American Marathon years and years ago; it's always been the most international of marathons. New York certainly has more international competitors in terms of volume because the race itself is so much larger. But in terms of international interest, Boston has always been at the forefront because it used to be the only game in town 20, 30, 40 years ago. So the heritage and the tradition were there and it continues to bring the world's best here year after year."

Morse was the race director in 1986, at the start of the increased presence of signage, advertising, attention, prize money, and other additions.

"When we instituted the whole prize-money structure and really aggressively recruited the elite athletes, we also thought, when we did that, that we needed to continue to make the race and the environment around the race the best that it can be in terms of conditions for the athletes," he recalled. "So we structured the media requests and the other appearances that they make, all to be in tune with what they need to do to prepare for the race because that's their primary motivation—that's their primary objective—to be the best that they can be in terms of preparation for the race on Monday."

Among the media ceremonies for the Boston Marathon is the presentation of bibs to the top participants—either defending champions, the previous year's top returnees, or via top times—as seen here in 2019 with, *from left*, Tatyana McFadden, Desiree Linden, Yuki Kawauchi, and Marcel Hug. *Photo by Paul Clerici.*

One of the elite athletes drawn to the newfound prize money and associated attraction was Australian Olympian Rob de Castella, the eventual 1986 Boston champion.

"It wasn't quite the big event it is today, but Hancock had a good handle on it all," he recalled. "Boston was quite behind the other marathons of the time, but Hancock knew what needed to be done and there was a commercial agenda in place as well. The media were, I recall, well supported and looked after. There were press conferences before and press conferences after, but I think it was a little bit separate from the BAA. Now there's much closer integration between [the sponsor] and the BAA."

In 1996, for its centennial, drastic measures were required not only to accommodate the ambitious field of 38,708 official entrants—a massive jump from the 9,416 the year before—but also to provide the media with superior services and the viewing audience with an equally high-quality product. To that end, a number of technological advances and several changes were instituted, including the replacement of the chute system of controlling the participants (to have them remain in line when they finish in order to record their bib numbers and places) with the use of ChampionChip technology (via a small transponder on the running shoes and wired mats on the ground).

"I recall in 1994 or 1995, prior to the 100th when we would have such a much greater participation, we had a real concern as to how are we going to process that many runners with that chute system," noted Morse. "At that time, that was still the norm. The chip technology was just beginning to appear. It saved us because we were able to officially process 38,000 finishers, which had never been done before. The numbers, even for the majors, the big-city marathons at that time, weren't that large. Talk about throwing it all in there. But it worked out well. And that's allowed the media to do a much better job covering the event, providing accurate and timely information to the viewers and to the public in general."

Spanning miles of road, thousands of runners, and continuous data, it was only a matter of time before digital technology made its way to Marathon coverage.

"They had this new digital equipment where it doesn't require this line-of-sight technology—it's not that old analog," said Reavis of the change. "It's much more clear. It's a better signal, a tighter signal, a stronger signal. It's like more bandwidth and you can put more information through it. They're not dependent on helicopters anymore."

For the first time, the 2005 Boston benefited from complete digital technology (which eventually led to other advances, such as the BAA

Racing App and mobile apps for tracking participants, web platforms and downloadable options, and the 2020 Boston Marathon Virtual Experience for that race-less year due to the COVID-19 pandemic).

"The new thing at Boston [in 2005 was] we're not using helicopters with microwave capabilities. Now it's digital," said Morse. "That technology is sufficient now that it can be done reasonably inexpensively, although it's still very expensive. But it's worth it because you can get a much better-quality signal and you get a more reliable signal."

With an amalgamation of better knowledge, greater technology, separate starts, and an overall symbiosis of additions and improvements, television coverage of Boston has continued and will continue to reach new heights.

"It's always been covered in a variety of ways," Morse said. "But the technology has really allowed the coverage to mature, along with the organization, frankly. Everything from the wireless opportunities now—the cellphones for tracking, for helping reporters out along the course, and just within the race itself—this is a benefit to all marathons, the whole chip technology and the tracking as well, which carries on the wireless system. The chip technology has allowed the media and the spectators to really understand what's going on [along] the course and to track it, almost immediately, from start to finish."

Samuelson has competed and traveled around the world and has seen many of the advances, both as competitor and commentator.

"I think as science and technology advance, so do other factors that come into play for the marathon and become more important, more recognized, by the press and the people following the marathon," she said.

Putting this all together also aided that cleanup of the roads, so to speak, in regard to the police motorcycles and official vehicles on the course. Tech-powered pool coverage, in particular, has enhanced the running, organizing, and viewing pleasure.

"Our pool television process now is accepted by everybody, so all three networks, for example, aren't vying for space on the [press] truck and they're not vying for vehicles on the course. It's just one set for sanity and safety," said Morse. "The technology allows them to get the information accurately and at the same time, so they can cooperate because it works for them. So that's helped us immensely as well. And they all supplement the on-course visuals with their own camera locations elsewhere and commentators as well for those broadcasting live."

Coverage on the Boston course includes a photo truck with a layered platform for print photographers and a press truck preceding each race.

Jordan Hasay finishing third at the 2019 Boston Marathon in front of a wall of photographers. *Photo by Paul Clerici.*

"The closest vehicle to the runners is the television truck. Only one," Morse explained, "with some motorcycle support, state police, et cetera, for security purposes. But those are burning natural gas. We have done a great job of eliminating the smog and the smoke and things of that nature. On the trucks, there're probably eight [people]. It's the representatives of all the live coverage of the race. It's purely press, purely media, and it's purely work. And then we have about 60 to 70 countries carrying it as well, and they all feed off the pool feed—the world feed, as we call it. It's all mixed in our trucks, which are in the corner of Boylston and Exeter [Streets] in the television alley there. It's just a huge operation."

Samuelson appreciates these changes, too. "It used to be pretty bad, the exhaust," she said. "Now, the distances are adequate enough between the runners and the vans, and the exhaust systems have improved. It's a lot better. It really isn't a factor now. There were…other marathons and other road races where you wanted to hold back because you didn't want to be breathing that belched air."

With the benefit of improved course infrastructure, more knowledgeable media personnel, advanced technology, expanding fields, and increasing interest from participants, the BAA constantly endeavors to stay ahead of the surges and provide improvements with the institution of several wide-ranging media press conferences.

As the Boston Marathon began—with an average of fewer than 50 entrants over the first nine years; first hitting 100 in 1906 (with 105) and 400 in 1964 (with 403)—there was no real need for highly organized press conferences. The race continued to remain manageable, as it took 72 years before the field first reached 1,000 entrants (1968), and it averaged only 2,700 in the 1970s (low of 1,067 in 1971; high of 7,929 in 1979) and 6,400 in the 1980s (low of 4,904 in 1986; high of 7,647 in 1982).

"Just like there weren't the numbers of runners that there are today, there weren't the number of press either," said Morse. "I think all the bib numbers were brought out to the start, like every other road race [then]. They were just given their numbers. I think [race official John] 'Jock'

At the 1951 Boston Marathon, reporters gather informally to interview, *from left*, runner-up John Lafferty, wreath-wearing champion Shigeki Tanaka, and third-place finisher Athanasios Ragazos. *Courtesy of the Boston Public Library, Leslie Jones Collection.*

Semple would give them the once-over to make sure they looked healthy to him—otherwise, they didn't get their number," he laughed. "There was a much less dramatic approach back then. There was no press conference, per se, and there weren't that many media around. And they weren't allowed in that room, I believe, out in Hopkinton, so they didn't catch up with the athletes until they finished."

And as Boston Marathon winners in the 1970s and '80s were primarily local athletes—Boston natives; Boston running and track club members; New Englanders—it was not uncommon to see the likes of Johnny "The Elder" Kelley (1935, 1945), Johnny "The Younger" Kelley (1957), Burfoot (1968), wheelchair winner Bob Hall (1975, 1977), Rodgers (1975, 1978, 1979, 1980), Alberto Salazar (1982), and Greg Meyer (1983) around the Hub on a regular basis. That accessibility benefited the media throughout the year.

"Hell, we lived with them!" exclaimed Reavis. "I used to live on Beacon Street [in Boston], two blocks from Bill Rodgers's store, so I would walk up every day and run with him. I lived it. Plus, they were mostly American kids, so I followed the sport year-round. These were American kids and I'd see them all throughout the races. And then I'd call up the international runners. It was actually easier. There were fewer athletes [and] you knew them better."

Pulitzer Prize–winning *Boston Globe* newspaper journalist and award-winning veteran sportswriter John Powers, who has covered Boston and the Olympics for decades, also enjoyed that easy access. One of the best spots was the now-defunct Eliot Lounge, a "sports" bar inside the Eliot Hotel, about a mile from the finish line, in which runners of all kinds would gather, including Boston winners from the Greater Boston Track Club (GBTC) such as Bob Hall, Meyers, Rodgers, and Salazar.

"The first several years I covered it, it was just a [one-]day event. If you wanted to talk to someone like Billy Rodgers, you did it. The clearinghouse back then was the Eliot Lounge, really," he noted. "You went there because that's where they were—[GBTC coach] Bill Squires, Rodgers—because back then they were all usually [GBTC] guys. There wasn't the national or international presence like there is now."

Rodgers, who also owned several Bill Rodgers Running Center stores in and around Boston, did try to accommodate the media whenever he could.

"It was intense," he said. "I always did a lot with the media and they would be calling me all the time. They'd call me at home, they'd come up to my house, I'd meet them at my store, I'd go to the [TV and radio] studio.

Four-time Boston Marathon champion Bill Rodgers being interviewed on camera. *Photo by Paul Clerici.*

I was into it—that's the way I am. I'm a marathoner and that was the deal. I do love the sport and it was fun. It didn't bother me, but there were some times I did get a little tired and I'd have to go back [home]."

When in 1965 the finish line moved from Exeter Street to Ring Road—an accessway parallel to Boylston Street in front of the Prudential Center—the BAA included a small press area nearby. A podium at the finish (and later at John Hancock Hall) was also added for the wreath, medal, and trophy presentations and the playing of the national anthems. The official setup (for 21 years, until it moved in 1986) for postrace interviews also ranged from asking questions on Ring Road, the parking garage, and even a barbershop inside the Pru, where Jack Fultz recalls the hectic minutes after his 1976 "Run for the Hoses" win in the blistering heat.

"After they put the wreath and medal on me and the five minutes of fanfare and photos out by the finish, they escorted me in and sat me down in a barber chair in a barbershop in the Prudential. They put a baby in my lap—the barber's grandchild for a photo op—and I sat there and answered questions for half an hour. And they gave me a big trophy from the [Massachusetts] Podiatry Society, I remember that," he said with a laugh. "You sit in a barber chair and it's like a little throne. By the time I got back out of the chair after sitting there for 45 minutes, I couldn't move. My legs had all stiffened up. But I was fine. I went out for a little run the next day. And of course, my whole life changed."

Powers also recalls the casual approach during those Ring Road days.

"The first year that Billy Rodgers won, 1975, we were at the barbershop at the Pru and he sat down in the barber chair. There were about a half-dozen of us [media] there and only about a handful of [elite runners] were coming in," he said. "Then they moved us in the Pru on a ramp to the garage. I remember in 1980 when Rosie Ruiz 'won,' we were on a ramp that went down to the garage. They had some tables and chairs set up and I remember that's when we met Rosie and she asked us who were we. And we asked her, 'Who are you?' Only the top few people were there. I remember we also talked to guys in the medical tent. When Beardsley and Salazar ran each other into the ground [in 1982], we talked to Salazar while he was hooked up to an IV!"

Three-time Colombian Olympian Alvaro Mejia fondly recalls fielding inquiries from the media at the Pru and elsewhere when he won Boston in 1971.

"They call me at home, yeah, and then they call me all the time and I was in all the papers in the United States," he recollected. "When I wake up, I go and bought all the newspapers [when I was] here in Boston, so I have all my papers."

With the infusion of John Hancock sponsor money in 1986, the finish line moved up Boylston Street, to near the Boston Public Library, closer to the former John Hancock Tower (farther away from the competing insurance company Prudential). With the move came a more structured schedule of media events within the days leading up to the race. The main additions were the John Hancock Elite Athlete Program Media Conference on the Friday before the race and the BAA Champions' Breakfast on Saturday. From these multi-hour media conferences originates the majority of the newspaper and magazine articles and photos, news and television footage, interviews, sound bites, and stories seen throughout race weekend.

At the Friday event, the media are seated as the invited elite athletes parade into the Fairmont Copley Plaza Hotel's 3,829-square-foot Oval Room to the small stage facing the assembled. At first, a select athlete or two—usually the defending champions, and for a time Rodgers as ambassador—spoke on behalf of the field.

"The first few years we asked a few of the athletes to speak in that setting and there wasn't the separate opportunity for interviews," recalled Morse. "That evolved where to meet the needs of the press, we pulled back on the speeches by the athletes in the formal setting and set them up ultimately by

The Fairmont Copley Plaza Hotel hosts many of the Boston Marathon events, including the main elite athlete media conference in its Oval Room. *Photo by Paul Clerici.*

country [at table seatings] and it became a two-part press conference. The media seems to love that because it gives them an opportunity to ask the questions one-on-one. And the athletes can answer all the questions, and when it's over, it's over."

Podium speakers transitioned to BAA and principal sponsor representatives, who welcome and address the room. Athletes then find their assigned tables along the perimeter of the Oval Room and adjacent 2,068-square-foot Venetian Room adorned by their respective country's flag.

"I think all of us who put on events like this understand that athletes have their own rhythm that they need to be able to follow to get ready to do their very best, and it's our job to help enable them to do the best they can," said former BAA executive director Tom Grilk. "So when it comes to the structuring of these events, we ask them, 'What would be best for you?' And [we] try to provide for them the structure that will allow them to be the best competitors they can be."

A couple hours of seemingly hectic, yet somewhat organized, rush ensues when hundreds of media members question the collected talent.

"I don't mind," said South African–born two-time Ireland Olympian Alistair Cragg. "Sometimes answering questions clears your thoughts. You're talking about things you talk to yourself [about] more times than you talk to other people, so I don't mind being bugged. This is handy. It's nice to get it out of the way."

Ryan Hall, who won the 2008 U.S. Olympic Trials Marathon and finished 10th in the Beijing Olympic Games Marathon, was 3rd at the 2009 Boston. "It's good," he said of the media conferences. "You just get it all done and then you can clear your mind and just get ready for the race and stay focused."

Desiree Linden, who won the 2018 Boston after a runner-up finish in 2011, also favors this method.

"It is good because it can kind of be drawn out for days if you don't have it all at once and [you can] say, 'All right, this is it. When it's done, it's done.' You get it done and you know you're going to be there for however long and you're excited about that because that's what you want to do—to talk to everyone and tell them how things went," she explains. "But then you do want to focus on your race, so it's nice that it's all done in a chunk like that. I think it just fits better because you can be more present and ready to be answering questions, whereas if someone calls me [another day], it'll be, like, a half-ass interview because I'm not prepared for that. I think you get a better answer when you're ready for it. I think it's better for both parties."

Three-time New Zealand Olympian Kim Smith also appreciated this kind of setup.

"The last couple of weeks [leading up to the Boston Marathon], I've had a few different interviews in a few different places as well, and it's nice to get them all out of the way. Then it's just about relaxing and keeping calm. It's nice to focus on the race," she said. "Marathons usually have some kind of press conference. [Boston] is pretty big compared to the other ones I've done, but usually they try and make sure that you're not going to be bothered the days before the race."

Some media see the single setting as the answer, as it provides direct face-to-face time. Hughes uses the opportunity as much as possible.

"The Friday press conference is a good opportunity to meet the athletes, to get a sense of their demeanor and focus, and to put the names with the faces. I appreciate that the speaking program is brief and that most of the time is devoted to individual question-and-answer sessions," she said. "Over the years, the BAA has provided more access to the athletes and opportunities to get to know them before race day. For example, if an athlete visits Boston before the race, the BAA provided us with interview opportunities and, often,

Boston Marathon media conference at the Fairmont Copley Plaza Hotel Grand Ballroom, with emcee U.S. Olympian Carrie Tollefson on stage *(far right)*. *Photo by Paul Clerici.*

a chance to shoot footage of the training run. With so much excitement and reverence for the Boston Marathon, the BAA has done a masterful job of expanding its reach—into initiatives, events, celebrations—that allow more people to feel a part of it."

Others in the media, for various reasons, see it as an impossible task to talk to everyone.

"The format for us in the press conference—20, 30 athletes in two hours—it's impossible," noted Reavis. "You can't talk to everybody. I don't particularly enjoy the system that's in place. In the old days, it was just more organic. We were lucky in having people like Billy [Rodgers] in the old days who was very outgoing and very well spoken and was a good talker and he liked to talk about it. It's difficult to get really good information [now]. But I have a good relationship with the coaches and the managers."

Planning for coverage obviously begins weeks and months beforehand, so the BAA accommodates that as well.

"If I need to talk to someone one-on-one, like the defending champion, it'll be arranged [for] after the press conference and they'll bring them in," Powers pointed out. "With the BAA, about a week before the press

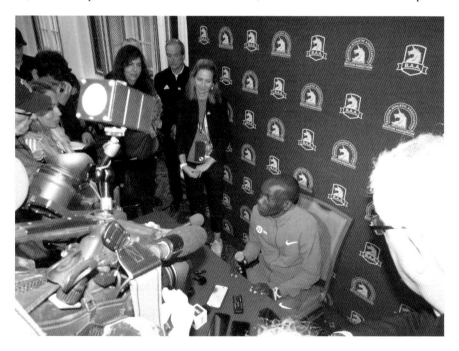

Two-time Olympic Marathon gold medalist and multiple record-holder Eliud Kipchoge of Kenya at a 2023 Boston Marathon media conference. *Photo by Paul Clerici.*

conferences, I'll say what I need for the features we're doing and I'll ask, for example, when are the Kenyans coming in, and we'll meet in the conference center. We'll work around their schedules and we'll meet there in case a translator is needed. That works."

As an elite runner with global credentials, de Castella understood the media demands and was prepared for what was expected of him when he came to Boston.

"As a professional athlete, you have an obligation to promote the event, recognize and acknowledge the sponsors, and be there to support what it's all about. That's part of your job," he noted. "I think most of the sports journalists that covered the Marathon had a reasonable respect for the athletes in terms of their preparation. You've got to be accessible, but you don't want that to be abused. And if you do have a journalist who abuses it, then the next time they call you, you're less inclined to be available or you don't give as good an interview. So it goes both ways. It's never been a major issue for me. It never worried me."

Media attention for Culpepper has always been in his life, from his high school state title-winning days to his All-American collegiate running to his experience at the U.S. Olympic Trials and two Olympic Summer Games.

"For me, growing up where I did in El Paso [Texas], there weren't any professional sports, so they followed high school-level athletics a lot. I've always had to do a lot of interview-type things even at an early age. Getting off the plane [from competitions] when I was 16 years old, the news [reporters] would be at the airport. Things like that. You get used to it and you get better at it. That's never really bothered me," he said. "It's always been a part of it, especially for the marathon. It's always been like, 'This is the structure and here's what you're going to have to do and this is the reason that we're able to have prize money and we're able to have the support.' [It's] because of these other aspects, the media outlets and the other aspects, that build up the event. I'm used to it. It's a positive thing, for sure, but it is a balance. It can certainly become a distraction and it can diminish what you're trying to really do, which is run the race. For me, like [at the Saturday press conference], this is appropriate because we still have a few more days till the race. The closer we get, the less I want to talk about it with the guy walking down the street or with a reporter. For me, it's just a balance of that."

Despite the convenience, there were some elite athletes who would rather be elsewhere than within the scheduled confines of even the one short media conference.

"I remember some other runners, like [Toshihiko] Seko, and he didn't want to hear it. He wanted to get the heck out of there," recalled Rodgers of the two-time Boston winner from Japan. "He'd be there for a little bit and then, 'I'm done.' But I think because I lived here, I could just go home. He was halfway around the world from home. It's tougher. But back then, I was in some room with about five or eight of the top runners in those days; they didn't bring everyone in like now. And there would be media there and I would do quite a lot of pre-race interviews. There would be one day that was the main day, but not as well defined with all the tables by country [like now]. But today it's much more structured and I think that's a good idea. The athletes have to rest. There's plenty of time to talk later, after the race."

Forty-eight hours before the gun, a more casual and celebratory event is held by the BAA in the Fairmont Copley Plaza Hotel Oval Room. Celebrated as the BAA Champions' Breakfast, the program includes top-bib presentations and brief questions and answers as well as nods to previous winners and race notables. But while the Saturday morning before the Marathon always held a BAA-sponsored media event in some form, it wasn't always as defined and refined.

"We used to have a press conference on Saturday morning to really call the press together. It would be a press-focused event, as opposed to a gathering of the clan. More of a photo op," explained Grilk. "The bib presentations were more like a press conference on Saturday morning, and that's evolved into the reunion/Champions' Breakfast where, yes, we make a formal presentation of the number 1 bibs to the returning champions, but as much as that [we also] bring back together the running community and as much of the history as we can find on two feet."

Powers, who first covered Boston in 1973, recalls that the smaller scale enabled Semple to make one-man decisions, and there was no outcry for large media conferences.

"Basically, if you wanted to run in the Boston Marathon, you called Jock at the old Boston Garden [office]. I was with him when he got a call and he would ask about your mile times and races. If you couldn't convince him you were a runner, you couldn't get in," said Powers with a chuckle. "And you could fit everyone [of the media] in one small bus. It was basically only the *Globe* and the *Boston Herald*, so for years there was no real call for them."

Elite bibs, which currently feature names for winners, were then numbered roughly based on seeding. Fultz, who several years after his 1976 win was the elite-athlete liaison for the BAA, explains the process by which numbers were assigned.

Above: Boston Marathon Champions Breakfast gathering in 2005, *from left*: Bill Rodgers, Lameck Aguta, Jacqueline Gareau, Doroteo Flores, wheelchair winner Bob Hall, Keizo Yamada, Uta Pippig, Amby Burfoot, Lisa Larsen-Weidenbach, women's wheelchair winner Jean Driscoll, Jack Fultz, and Johnny "The Younger" Kelley. *Photo by Paul Clerici.*

Opposite, top: At the 2011 Boston Marathon Champions Breakfast ceremony, *from left*: Jean Driscoll, Rob de Castella, Alvaro Meija, and Ron Hill. *Photo by Paul Clerici.*

Opposite, bottom: Boston Marathon race-day media room at the Fairmont Copley Plaza Hotel Oval Room. *Photo by Paul Clerici.*

"What they did then and continued to do all the way up through the late '80s and early '90s when I was the liaison was the seeding process where anybody that returned who had finished in the top 50 got the bib number that equated to their finishing place. And then all the ones that were left open got put in by a subjective seeding process by what they ran," he pointed out. "I had the lucky number 14 in 1976. That was Bill Rodgers's number in 1975, and I think number 14 [won again with Johnny Miles in 1926 and Bob Hall in 1975]."

The other main feature of the BAA Champions' Breakfast—the recognition and reunion of past winners and notables—began in earnest at the centennial Boston in 1996. That seminal celebration drew more than 40 previous champions.

"Saturday morning, which was the traditional BAA press conference that has gone back decades even before [I started in 1984]," noted Morse, "was retooled so that it was more of a breakfast—a little bit more informal—and as it continues, we hope to get it more and more informal. We also made it the reunion, if you will, for the athletes. The BAA breakfast has really become a focal point and important not only to the elite athletes for the presentation of numbers but also to all the returning champions. That's because this event, more than any other event, I think, has that fraternity of past winners and it has become an annual meeting, if you will, for the elite of today and the elite of the past. It's a very, very important event."

On race day itself, eons from the time of communication via walkie-talkies and transistor radios, the Oval and Venetian Rooms, and on occasion the 6,090-square-foot Grand Ballroom, host the media with rows of seats, Internet and digital connections, monitors showing the races live, and real-time race info. With these media services, since the immediacies of instant reporting are involved, the Boston Marathon Race Day Press Conference

BAA Wrap-Up Media Conference the day after the 2019 race with John Hancock assistant vice president Rob Friedman (*center*), alongside winners, *from left*: Manuela Schar, Lawrence Cherono, Daniel Romanchuk, and Worknesh Degefa. *Photo by Paul Clerici.*

also features athlete interview opportunities. That is followed later that evening by the BAA Awards Ceremony, which is open to the public.

And then the day after the race is held the Boston Marathon Champions Wrap-up Media Conference, or BAA Wrap-up Media Conference, also at the Fairmont Copley Plaza Hotel. It provides another chance to interview the winners and also for the BAA to provide any updates or state-of-the-race information. In addition, photo ops of the big (as in physical size and monetary worth) checks for wins and records are presented. This gathering can particularly benefit the local news stations and weekly and monthly newspapers more than the dailies.

MONUMENTS AND STATUES

The Boston Marathon runs in Hopkinton, Ashland, Framingham, Natick, Wellesley, Newton, Brighton, Brookline, and Boston. Via monuments, statues, or memorials, communities have their own identity and personal nod to the historic race.

"I would venture a guess," surmised former Boston Marathon race director Tim Kilduff, "there's no other marathon in the world that pays as much attention to the history and the historical significance that running a marathon represents, than Boston."

For its first 27 years (1897–1923), Boston started in the MetroWest region of Ashland. The first two editions started on Pleasant Street, along the Boston and Albany Railroad tracks, near Metcalf's Mill. From 1899 to 1906, the start was about three-tenths of a mile west, on the High Street bridge over the train tracks. And from 1907 to 1923, the start was in the area of Valentine farm, on Hopkinton Road at Steven's Corner, near the current 4K (2.48 miles) mark of the race.

Massachusetts Senate president Karen Spilka recognizes the importance of the race's origins and is especially proud of it since her district includes many of the communities on the course.

"I think the MetroWest is the place to be for the Marathon. Most people, when they think Boston Marathon, they think Boston; I think of Hopkinton, Ashland, Framingham, Natick, that are all in my district, towards Boston," she noted. "The original part, the beginning part of the Marathon, is out here in MetroWest. The history of the start is out here

Detailed plaques of the Boston Marathon during its 27 years in Ashland, from 1897 to 1923. *Photo by Paul Clerici.*

in MetroWest. And I think that it's really important that we celebrate the towns. And it's wonderful that Hopkinton and Ashland are working together to celebrate [where] it all started and [where] it all starts—it's all the same thing. It's the whole sport of marathoning and what it stands for—the strength, the persistence, as well as what the original marathon symbolized as well back in Greece. I think it's important to continue to celebrate that connection."

The original site has experienced various landscaped additions. One of the first signs—the only one for decades—was a literal sign, nailed to a tree, that declared, "Welcome to Ashland. It All Started Here in 1897. Ashland to Boston 25 Miles."

"Recognizing and celebrating Ashland's contribution to the Boston Marathon has really been understated," said Kilduff, also president of the Hopkinton nonprofit 26.2 Foundation. "When you really think about the fact the Boston Athletic Association (BAA) instituted this long-distance race [based] after the first Modern Olympic Marathon in 1896, and trying to replicate a course that was similar to the one in Athens, they looked at a lot of other sites—like going to Concord—and they came west. The critical element was the train line coming out to Ashland. Its historic value has

Top: Site of the original Boston Marathon start on Pleasant Street in Ashland, marked by two traffic cones, where the race began in 1897 and 1898. *Photo by Paul Clerici.*

Bottom: Marathon Park at the Pleasant Street location of the first Boston Marathon, which was held in 1897 in Ashland. *Photo by Paul Clerici.*

gotten lost. There were a lot of us in Hopkinton that felt it was appropriate for us to create a celebration to honor our neighbors."

Eventually, the vacant mill site was redesigned as Marathon Park, with monuments, plaques, walkways, and signage depicting facts about the likes of early torchbearers as newspaper sports editor Jerry Nason, race timer Tony Nota, and race official John "Jock" Semple; early champions John McDermott, Frederick Lorz, Thomas Longboat, Clarence DeMar, and Bill Kennedy; the World War I-era relay champion Camp Devens Division Team of 1918; and more.

"There are people that come along every so often who get a spark—they think a little bit about it and get an appreciation for what came before them—and that's how that park was built. It's been literally built brick by brick," stated Kilduff. "And the 26.2 Foundation is going to continue to bring light on the Ashland contribution to the Marathon and we're bringing others in and around that story—for example, the MetroWest Boston Visitors Bureau—and focus on the MetroWest piece of the Boston Marathon. One of the secrets of the Boston Marathon is the course itself. When people come here from out of the region, it's the Boston Marathon and they forget about what precedes that [logistically]. If you include Wellesley as part of MetroWest/Boston, half the race is in MetroWest. There are those of us that live out here and were born and raised here and work here that are committed to making sure that people don't forget that this is a 26.2-mile course and a substantial portion runs through these communities that we call MetroWest."

BAA CEO and president Jack Fleming has always cherished the town's importance.

"You can't get to Boston without going through Ashland! We know the pride that [Ashland] takes in having a big part of it," he said. "At Marathon Park, you can really feel—you can, really feel—the spirit there, the heritage there; Sudbury River, railroad tracks, trees—you can feel the history. It's beautiful. [I thank] Ashland for keeping that important location alive, remembered, preserved, and maintained for all of our runners [now] and for future runners and for those who just want to visit. You can really feel the inspiration blowing in the wind there. It really doesn't get any more authentic than that."

At the 1908 London Olympic Games, the marathon distance increased from 40K (24.85 miles) to 42K (26.2 miles) so the royal family could view both the start at Windsor Castle and the finish at the royal box inside White City Stadium. When that distance became universal, Boston's starting line moved westward to Hopkinton in 1924.

Top: *Keepers of the Flame* monument at Marathon Park in Ashland. *Photo by Paul Clerici.*

Bottom: B25 stone marker, located just off Pleasant Street in Ashland, signifying the approximate start line and distance of the first Boston Marathon in 1897. *Photo by Paul Clerici.*

"This race is so much about the history and tradition…and you begin to marvel at the fact that you are running on the same hallowed ground as all these iconic runners once did," observed Boston Marathon race director Dave McGillivray, who first ran the race in 1973. "Nothing else like it in the world."

Hopkinton Town Common is the site of several monuments to the race. In addition to the perennial "It All Starts Here" sign is a permanent ground-level plaque at the intersection of its two brick-laid pathways—Johnny Kelley Crossing. It honors Johnny "The Elder" Kelley, the two-time U.S. Olympian who won Boston in 1935 and 1945, started the race a record 61 times, and finished a record 58.

A street sign on the access road that connects East Main Street and Ash Street designates Marathon Way. And at the northeast corner of Ash Street and Marathon Way, on a 10-inch-high, 16-square-foot granite base, is the 2008 Michael Alfano–created *The Starter* statue, an 80-inch-tall bronze of George V. Brown, precisely situated on the start line extended.

"George was born and lived his life in the town, was instrumental in moving the starting line to Hopkinton, and served as starter of the Boston Marathon for nearly 30 years, having been involved since just after its inception," said Alfano. "We reviewed photos of George Brown and the early races and decided to depict him starting the race. We placed the sculpture at the starting line to serve as a yearlong commemoration to it and to be a spot where people could pose with it as if they were starting the race, especially for photos. Many visitors to the town throughout the year do just that, and probably thousands do so every year on race weekend."

On Ash Street is the Mike Tabor–created *Yes You Can!* statue of the late father-son Team Hoyt duo of Dick Hoyt, who pushed his son Rick Hoyt, born with cerebral palsy and diagnosed a spastic quadriplegic. They competed in over 1,100 events, including 6 Ironman triathlons and more than 70 marathons, including Boston 32 times together.

"I feel so honored to be a part of history like the other bronze statues that have been made before me," communicated Rick Hoyt on his specialized computer via assistance from his personal care assistant Jessica Gauthier. "My dad and me (along with my mom) have helped pave the pathway for other families with disabilities, and I am hoping people will also see that when they look at the bronze statue. I never thought I would have had a statue made of us. It is truly an honor."

In regard to the statue's 2013 dedication, Dick Hoyt was especially emotional.

Top: Hopkinton Town Common with the iconic "It All Starts Here" sign—courtesy of the Hopkinton Marathon Committee— and U.S. Olympic Marathon gold and silver medalist Frank Shorter (*bottom left*). *Photo by Paul Clerici*.

Bottom: *Johnny Kelley Crossing* at the intersection of two walkways at Hopkinton Town Common. *Photo by Paul Clerici*.

Top: Marathon Way, between Hopkinton Town Common and the Boston Marathon start line on East Main Street. *Photo by Paul Clerici.*

Bottom: *The Starter* statue of George V. Brown in Hopkinton. *Photo by Paul Clerici.*

"It's an awesome feeling," he said. "I think back to when Rick was born and they said to put him away in an institution because he's going to be nothing but a vegetable for the rest of his life, and all the things that we've been able to accomplish. My 'vegetable,'" he said, holding back his emotions, "is now a bronze statue! I mean, how much better can it be? It can't be any better."

At the Korean Presbyterian Church in Greater Boston, 2 Main Street in Hopkinton, on the front lawn is a flat, 16-square-foot, gray marble monument that is slightly hidden from street-level view due to it rising only inches from the ground. In its center is a black outline of Korea over a colored yin and yang version of the Stars and Stripes. Encircling the design are Korean race results, some names and times of which differ from their listing in U.S. sources, and "Boston Marathon 1903-2003 Korean-American Centennial." To commemorate the 100th anniversary of Korean immigration, the Douglas Duksoo Wohn–designed monument was dedicated in 2004 by the New England Centennial Committee of Korean Immigration to the U.S. and donated by the church.

Also in Hopkinton, slightly behind the start line, at the east corner of Main Street and Hayden Rowe Street, is *The Girl Who Ran* statue. Honoring

Flat monument, dedicated in 2004 in Hopkinton at the Korean Presbyterian Church in Greater Boston, to commemorate the 100th anniversary of Korean immigration to America, features the top Korean finishers of the Boston Marathon (1947, 1950, 2001). *Photo by Paul Clerici.*

Yes You Can! statue of Team Hoyt on Ash Street in Hopkinton of Dick Hoyt pushing his son Rick Hoyt. *Photo by Paul Clerici.*

runner, artist, and sculptor Roberta "Bobbi" Gibb, the first woman to finish the Boston Marathon—which she did in 1966—it was created and unveiled in 2021 by the subject herself.

"It was really weird doing [a statue of] myself. I wanted to do a generic one and Tim [Kilduff] said, 'No, we're hiring you to do one of you.' And I said, 'Oh, my god! I can't do that.' So then [while working on it] I'm looking at my leg, I'm looking at my arm—it was the first time I had a live model," she said with a laugh. "It was truly weird. But I remember [wearing in 1966] my brother's Bermuda shorts and a tank-top bathing suit. It was so much fun doing a life-size one."

Among her creations are the 12-inch bronze Olympia female figurine trophies that were awarded at the 1984 U.S. Olympic Women's Marathon Trials.

"When I do a sculpture, it has to be alive, whether it's a portrait, a bust—it has to catch the person when I do it. I do a lot of motion. I don't think I've ever done someone standing still; it's all running, athletes running. I do it out of my own head. I don't have a model because who's going to stand there and run," she laughed. "I visualize it. I feel it from the inside and then I put it into the bronze, so it has to be alive. And that's what I did with this one. She came out good."

Rodgers, who, along with his brother Charlie Rodgers, attended the unveiling ceremony, praises Gibb.

"We always believed in Roberta Gibb," he said, "as she should be the 'First Woman of the Boston Marathon' because of her courage in breaking the rules. Sometimes rules need to be broken, if they're real backwards, which they were in regards to women running. And all us guy runners all felt the same way. But some of the officials didn't understand it because they were told by the [AAU] that if you allow women to run, 'you're going to lose your license to have your race.' That's ridiculous!"

Having the statue of Gibb near the physical spot where she began her journey at the 1966 Boston is most fitting.

"We all want to salute Roberta because one of the problems was it became unclear about who was the woman that really did the deal—it was Roberta, not anyone else," Rodgers stated. "Most people didn't [understand] and to this day don't understand that the first woman to run the Boston Marathon is Roberta Gibb. So we all salute Roberta."

At the one-mile mark of the course, on the donated grounds of the Weston Nurseries Garden Center at 93 East Main Street, is one of two *The Spirit of the Marathon* statues and the only one in the United States. Situated near a landform once known as Lucky Rock, close to where the Boston start

Athlete, artist, lawyer, scientific researcher, and author Roberta "Bobbi" Gibb with the 2021 *The Girl Who Ran* sculpture she was asked to create in honor of her being the first woman to finish the Boston Marathon, which she ran in 1966. *Photo by Paul Clerici.*

Left: *The Spirit of the Marathon* statue at the one-mile mark of the Boston Marathon course in Hopkinton. *Photo by Paul Clerici.*

Below: Base of *The Spirit of the Marathon* statue depicts the demigod Pan behind the mythical Greek messenger Pheidippides. *Photo by Paul Clerici.*

line was located decades ago, the 3,400-pound hollow bronze is 14 feet tall, including the base. Located on the left-hand side of the runners, the famous Greek runners depicted are 1896 Modern Olympic Marathon winner Spiridon Louis (on the right) and 1946 Boston winner Stylianos Kyriakides (on the left).

The original idea came from Kyriakides's co-biographer Nick Tsiotos. In 1997, a decade after Kyriakides died, the initial concept was for a single-figure statue of the Boston winner to honor his postwar efforts to raise awareness of his devastated country, which was in great need following World War II. His victory resulted in boatloads of supplies for his homeland, for which his son, Dimitri Kyriakides, is forever grateful.

"The statues help remind people of the story and for many other people to know the story after they see them. I now see Stylianos Kyriakides not as my father, but as a man, a human being that should be an example to all of us and to remind us all how we really should be if we want to make our world better," Dimitri Kyriakides said. "I have spent much time and personal resources for spreading the legacy of my father over the past [many] years because I think that it is a story that must be told and that must be remembered."

To join together Greece and the Boston Marathon, one statue was set for the original marathon finish in Athens—for the 2004 Olympic Games there—and the other for Hopkinton, both by Mico Kaufman, of Tewksbury, Massachusetts. But as Dimitri Kyriakides explained, it was a difficult journey to Greece.

"The story is a Greek tragedy," he said. "In 2000, the [Athens] mayor changed. In October 2001, we had the presentation of the book. In 2002, the Greek American delegation visited Athens and met [the new mayor who] told them that this is not possible and she will only accept the gift if they gave her one more statue [of Louis]. In 2003, [the mayor] changed her mind and said that she does not want the statue!"

So the vice mayor of Marathon (where the race finishes) agreed in writing to accept the statue and pay for transportation and installation. The original completion date of 2003 was now June 2004 due to the extra work involved with the additional figure of Louis.

"[The vice mayor then] told me that the city had no money to pay for the transportation! This was because of the late readiness [of] the statue that [it] could no longer arrive in time by sea freight but had to be transported by air," noted Dimitri Kyriakides. "The statue was in the customs warehouse [in Greece] and…it was just before the Olympics with so many equipment coming in the country and the warehouses full. [I was told] that if the statue was presented as a 'gift' from a Greek American society, then no import duty was needed. So [we] 'fabricated' a letter and the statue came out of customs, finally, with 10 days to spare before the start of the Games."

In Hopkinton, an identical statue was dedicated for the 2006 Boston. The top portion depicts a victorious Stylianos Kyriakides running the 1946 Boston alongside Louis in spirit, who is shown not earthbound, having died in 1940. On the east-facing side of the base is an image of Stylianos Kyriakides wearing his olive-branch wreath.

"The rocky hills of the base are the hills near the plain of Marathon, where the Greek army was based in 490 BC. And on [the west-facing] side is demigod Pan that assisted the Athenians to win—according to the myth. Pan lived in a cave in the hills near Marathon," said Dimitri Kyriakides, who added that the other figure on the base is Pheidippides, "who runs to Athens to announce the victory and then died."

In Newton, at about 19.1 miles on the course, is a statue of Johnny "The Elder" Kelley called *Young at Heart*, named after the 1953 Johnny Richards–Carolyn Leigh song made famous by Frank Sinatra that Kelley often sang. Located about 75 feet from the corner of Walnut Street and Commonwealth Avenue, on the left of the runners as they pass by during the race, the 1,500-pound, 7-foot-tall double-figure statue stands on top of a 40,000-pound 2-foot, 4-inch-tall granite base.

Initially named *Young at Heart: The Johnny Kelley Heartbreak Hill Heroic Sculpture* (as noted in the statue's dedication pamphlet), the two depictions of hand-holding Kelleys are of when he first won Boston in 1935 (on the left) and when he last ran Boston in 1992 (on the right). The twin-body idea came from Dr. Wayman R. Spence, who was chairman of the Johnny Kelley Sculpture Committee. According to his explanation in the dedication pamphlet, while working on a separate project Spence awoke from a dream in which he envisioned older and younger versions of Kelley running together. He subsequently commissioned Oklahoma sculptor Rich Muno.

The statue was dedicated the day before the 1993 Boston, and among those on hand were Kelley, Morse, Muno, Rodgers, Spence, and two-time defending Boston champion Ibrahim Hussein of Kenya. The statue was originally located near a street about a block eastward from its current site, at Bullough Park, on the other side of Walnut Street. It was moved to its present location shortly after the dedication.

"I would say no more than six months later—this was before the next Boston Marathon—a car hit the statue," recalled David Donahue of Tody's

Top: *Young at Heart* statue of two-time winner Johnny "The Elder" Kelley, on the course in Newton. *Photo by Paul Clerici*.

Bottom: The Massachusetts Avenue *Tommy Leonard Bridge*, less than a mile from the Boston Marathon finish, named in honor of the Official Greeter of the Boston Marathon. *Photo by Paul Clerici*.

Service Inc., the auto garage called on to clean up the accident scene and move the statue.

In the statue's initial spot, the Kelleys faced the oncoming runners of the Boston Marathon. After the statue was moved, it faced the hills in the same direction as the Marathon field. The process by which Tody's gently moved the 41,500-pound piece of art was itself a work of art.

"My father, Tody, said we have to drop it down, to the new spot, with the crane," recalled Donahue. He told [Newton Parks and Recreation manager Carol Stapleton] to get 10 bags of ice. It was suspended by nylon straps underneath and we placed it on the ice, positioned it, and when the ice melted, that's where you see it now."

The statue is visible from the course but can be difficult to see during the race due to its distance from the street. But no one will ever see one thing that was added during its move.

"I put a $10 bill underneath," Donahue said with a laugh. "Well, I was young and foolish back then. It was something to do. I always said that if you ever see Johnny Kelley on its side, that I needed the money."

Just over six miles farther west on the course, about three-tenths of a mile beyond Kenmore Square, is the Philip G. Bowker Overpass. Painted in 2016 in blue and yellow on the west side of the bridge, which connects Boylston Street and Storrow Drive, are the words *Boston Strong*. The public domain phrase, attributed to Emerson College students Christopher Dobens and Nicholas Reynolds, became the common reference source of survival pride after the 2013 Boston Marathon bombings.

Closer to the finish line, at about 25.5 miles, is the Massachusetts Avenue *Tommy Leonard Bridge* at the intersection of Commonwealth Avenue, in the shadow of the Eliot Hotel. The bridge was named in 1982 after the longtime bartender of the now-defunct famous runners bar Eliot Lounge, which was housed inside the hotel; the BAA had also honored Leonard with the title of "Boston Marathon Official Greeter" due to his decades-long devotion to and love of the race.

At one time, the course proceeded along Commonwealth Avenue over Massachusetts Avenue, with the bridge to the left of the runners. In 2006, the course changed to divert participants under Massachusetts Avenue and the *Tommy Leonard Bridge* and reappear on the main portion of Commonwealth Avenue a few hundred yards later, en route to the Hereford Street turn to Boylston Street and the finish.

"I was totally overwhelmed. It was a total surprise," said Leonard, who passed away in 2019, about the bridge naming. "They had hinted about it, but I thought they were joking. And they weren't. The City of Boston put on a big spread at the Eliot. I don't think I was worthy of it."

On Boyleston Street, at the two separate sites where pressure-cooker bombs were detonated during the 2013 race, stands the Boston Marathon Marker Memorial, by Bolivian-born Bay State sculptor Pablo Eduardo.

"The basic idea was to mark the physical spots where the bombs went off and make them special and beautiful so that they would become kind of holy," he noted. "We bumped out the curve and took out a few parking spaces to depict an area that was forever changed by what happened. We used materials that are common on the Back Bay, such as brick and stone. And incorporated casted glass and bronze to symbolize the fragility and strength of people and our ideals. The craftsmanship and detail had to be excellent to show our respect."

Dedicated in 2019, the two-piece monument includes such features as granite, stone, pillars, and illuminating bronze glass spires.

"We kept in mind the families of the victims always. We wanted the memorial to be made with love [for] the community to come together, to be a kind of [like a] lantern/beacon," Eduardo explained. "Most of [the involved commissions and groups] were very supportive, as we respected the area and we wanted to design something that belonged there. The design process was a little complicated because the whole thing was still so emotionally raw for the families. And who would say otherwise. We had to be very patient and caring and listen to what they wanted. A sacred, beautiful, small, and unassuming place, the design had to incorporate so many things and make them work together tightly; an example is how we incorporated granite from all over New England to symbolize all the people that come together here in Boston to run on the day of the Marathon bombing. I use the word 'symbol' perhaps too many times, but I feel that everything about this memorial was symbolic."

Eduardo was comforted by the talent around him who all maintained focus on the sacred honor.

"All the craftsmen and contractors, masons, material suppliers—everyone that took part—were very thankful that they were part of the creation. Everyone knew, I feel, the significance," he said. "It was always moving to see this every day. The memorial took a bit longer than anticipated because the lights were a little complicated to fabricate and we underestimated the time, but in the end it worked out for the better. I am enormously thankful that the City of Boston and the families of the victims entrusted me with the task. I hope I came through for everyone."

Lit spires of the Pablo Eduardo-created Boston Marathon Marker Memorial on Boylston Street. *Photo by Paul Clerici.*

Just beyond the finish line are two separate Marathon-related monuments in Copley Square Park, a public greenery one block east of the finish line and to the right of the runners as they walk down Boylston Street after they finish.

Detail of the *Boston Marathon Marker Memorial* on Boylston Street. *Photo by Paul Clerici.*

At the northwest corner of Boylston and Dartmouth Streets, about 100 feet behind the finish, is the seven-ton Boston Marathon Centennial Monument. It is in the shape of a flat, medallion-style, engraved circle 15 feet in circumference and marked by four opposing 40-inch pink marble

Boston Marathon Marker Memorial on Boylston Street. *Photo by Paul Clerici.*

bollards. Dedicated on April 9, 1996, in celebration of the race's centennial, it was created by landscape architect Mark Flannery and artists Robert Shure and the late Robert Lamb.

According to Gina Caruso, BAA licensing and special events coordinator at the time, the criteria for the design specified that it should "be sensitive to its setting in Copley Square; reflect the legendary history of the Marathon, if not explicitly then symbolically, such as using the laurel wreath; allow spaces for acknowledging winners of the Marathon, past, present, and future; have a universal appeal and recognition from athletes and all world visitors."

While the original accepted submission featured a large archway under which visitors could walk (eventually replaced by the marble posts), the final version includes the wreath, names, and the required symbiosis with its surroundings. It also had to be approved by nearly a dozen organizations, including the BAA, John Hancock Mutual Life Insurance Company, Boston Parks Commission, Boston Art Commission, and several other entities associated with Copley Square, all of this within 14 months, from creation to dedication!

Top: Boston Marathon Centennial Monument at Copley Square in Boston. *Photo by Paul Clerici.*

Bottom: Closeup of marble column of the *Boston Marathon Centennial Monument* at Copley Square in Boston. *Photo by Paul Clerici.*

Etched in the common area walkway is a two-tone map and elevation chart of the course comprising nine different pieces of granite and the names of every male and female overall, masters, and wheelchair winner. The monument is updated with each year's list of six new champions.

"I like the way they used different color stone for the elevation and the different towns that you went through," observed Gibb, one of the 10 chosen to pull back the tarp at its unveiling. "That was fun—pulling it back and seeing the course. It was very well done. I love the circle [of names, including hers] that can keep going out and out and pretty soon can take up the whole Square."

From 11 separate quarries are 42 pieces of granite, all but one engraved. On each three-foot marble post are reliefs by Shure and Lamb of the BAA's unicorn logo; a different aspect of the race (male runner; female runner; male and female winners; wheelchair athlete); and seals of each community of the course.

"I think it was very well conceived. I like the whole concept of it—the circle of time and the fact that it's flat," said Gibb. "They got all the symbols there. They put in all the towns, the different aspects of the race—wheelchair, the woman, the man—very well representative. A lot of variation that makes it interesting. Very imaginative. I thought it was a very great addition to the city landscape, actually, as well as a memorial. You see the care that went into it—a lot of careful thinking and careful execution."

And a short hop, skip, and jump toward Trinity Church and the 60-story former John Hancock Tower is the playful *Tortoise and Hare* statue, the slow-and-steady tale referenced in Aesop's Fables. Also dedicated in honor of the Marathon's centennial, it was installed nearly a year before, in May 1995. The two closely separated larger-than-life bronze animals—a 21x30x60-inch tortoise and a 22x33x50-inch hare—were created by Newton sculptor Nancy Schon, whose sculptures encourage the interaction of children.

ABOUT THE AUTHOR

Paul C. Clerici is the best-selling author of *Born to Coach: The Story of Bill Squires, the Legendary Coach of the Greatest Generation of American Distance Runners* (Meyer + Meyer Sport Publishers), *Oregon Running Legend Steve Prefontaine: In the Footsteps of the U.S. Olympic Athlete, Activist, and Icon* (The History Press), *Images of Modern America: The Boston Marathon* (THP), *A History of the Falmouth Road Race: Running Cape Cod* (THP), *Boston Marathon History by the Mile* (THP), *Journey of the Boston Marathon* (Cheers Publishing, China), and *History of the Greater Boston Track Club* (THP). He is a journalist, public speaker, media guest, documentary film contributor, writer, photographer, and former newspaper editor and sports editor recognized in the Marquis Who's Who in the East publications and received its Albert Nelson Marquis Lifetime Achievement Award. He has written for newspapers and magazines, including *Level Renner*, *Marathon & Beyond*, *Meter*, *New England Patriots Weekly*, *New England Runner*, *Orlando Attractions Magazine*, *Running Times*, and the *Walpole Times*, among them; and has produced shows at Walpole Community Television. A New England Press Association and Massachusetts Press Association award winner, he was also written for *Running Times/Runner's World*, *Strava*, and *Tracksmith Journal* websites and blogs. Race director of the Camy 5K Run & David 5K Walk, he has competed in nearly every distance from the mile to the marathon—including 2 triathlons and 43 marathons (the Boston Marathon 23 years in a row)—and has won several running age-group and Clydesdale awards. A graduate of Curry College in Milton, Massachusetts, the Walpole High School Hall of Fame member resides in his Massachusetts hometown.